Military Expenditure and Economic Growth in the Middle East

Military Expenditure and Economic Growth in the Middle East

Latif Wahid

palgrave
macmillan

First published 2009 by
PALGRAVE MACMILLAN

Palgrave Macmillan in the UK is an imprint of Macmillan Publishers Limited, registered in England, company number 785998, of Houndmills, Basingstoke, Hampshire RG21 6XS.

Palgrave Macmillan in the US is a division of St Martin's Press LLC, 175 Fifth Avenue, New York, NY 10010.

Palgrave Macmillan is the global academic imprint of the above companies and has companies and representatives throughout the world.

Palgrave® and Macmillan® are registered trademarks in the United States, the United Kingdom, Europe and other countries.

ISBN: 978–0–230–22017–1 hardback

This book is printed on paper suitable for recycling and made from fully managed and sustained forest sources. Logging, pulping and manufacturing processes are expected to conform to the environmental regulations of the country of origin.

A catalogue record for this book is available from the British Library.

A catalog record for this book is available from the Library of Congress.

10 9 8 7 6 5 4 3 2 1
18 17 16 15 14 13 12 11 10 09

Printed and bound in Great Britain by
CPI Antony Rowe, Chippenham and Eastbourne

Contents

Tables and Figures

Tables

Figures

Preface

Since the end of Britain and France's mandate in the first half of the last century, the Middle East has been afflicted with continuous military confrontations, wars, and political instability. As a consequence, the economic and social development of the region has been profoundly hindered. A disproportionate amount of the region's scarce resources have been allocated to war efforts and the strengthening of huge armies which have since dominated political life in the region. Prospects for regional economic development have subsequently been inhibited. On the other hand, the dominance of the military in most of the countries of the region has prevented modern social and civil institutions from developing, which has consequently deprived its people from benefiting from the advances of modern technology and globalisation. In addition, political instability has discouraged foreign investment and technological transfer into the region. As is well known, the region is well endowed with human and natural resources. It is also at the gateway to Europe, where the modern technological and industrial revolution was initiated. Despite all this, the Middle East has failed to harness the availability of these resources for the economic development and progress of its citizens. Authorities in the region are quick to apportion blame to foreign powers for the ills of their countries. Although foreign power rivalries in the region have played an important role in fuelling the almost uninterrupted state of war in the region, this book regards these regional authorities – and particularly the armed forces – as important players in creating the current adverse conditions. Military institutions have ruled the Middle East for far too long. They have fundamentally retarded its social and economic development and are largely responsible for the suffering of its people.

This book attempts to redress the approach to the underdevelopment of the Middle East by looking at the origins of conflicts and role of armed forces in the political and economic development of the region. It also looks at the economies of countries that have been affected by the military hostilities and discusses trends in military expenditure.

It is hoped that this book will encourage further research on the topic and strengthen the argument for peace and the democratic approach to conflict resolution. It is also written in a manner that makes it accessible to the wider public as well as to economic and political scholars in the area.

In writing this book, I am indebted to my colleague and friend Dr Sima Motamin-Samadian who has read parts of the book and offered valuable comments and encouragement. My ultimate thanks go to my family; my wife Asia Ramzi, my son Alan and my daughter Jala who coped with and tolerated my shortcomings during this endeavour.

Latif Wahid

To the memory of my brother Marif Karim Wahid (1964–1988) and other victims of the military and military regimes in the Middle East

1
Introduction

Since the collapse of the Ottoman Empire at the end of the First World War, the Middle East, unlike any other region of the world, has been afflicted with frequent military conflict, inter-state hostility and civil wars. Great Britain and France largely, and arbitrarily, carved the current states out of the former. The border demarcations of the states and international agreements were decided upon with no consideration of the wishes of the people of the region. Even the states' names, as Lewis (2003) points out, reflect their artificiality: Iran, Syria, Palestine and Libya are names from classical antiquity that haven't been used in the region for thousands of years and names such as Algeria, Tunisia and Arabia don't exist as words in Arabic. Most, if not all, current conflicts have, in some way or another, historical roots in the problems inherited in these colonial settings of the countries of the region.

Given the prevailing geopolitical conditions of the region, the prolonged economic stagnation that the region suffers from compared with the experience of the Latin American and the South East Asian economies comes to no surprise. It is a paradox that in addition to the abundant natural and human resources and the close proximity of the region to Europe, the region has benefited very little from the technological progress that Europe has harnessed in the last century and a half. While the South East Asian countries have progressed by leaps and bounds in the past 30 years or so, economic and social development in the Middle East remain marred by inefficient use of resources, poor governance, absence of foreign investment and unconstitutional and undemocratic governments.

The ramifications of the overall economic and political conditions for human development in the region have been immense. Table 1.1 shows that only five out of the 20 countries in the region are ranked by the

Table 1.1 MENA countries and the Human Development Index

HDI Rank	Country	Human Development Index							
		1975	1980	1985	1990	1995	2000	2002	2003
23	Israel	0.80	0.82	0.84	0.86	0.88	0.91	0.91	0.92
40	Qatar	–	–	–	–	–	–	0.83	0.85
41	UAE	0.73	0.77	0.79	0.81	0.80	–	0.82	0.85
43	Bahrain	–	0.75	0.78	0.81	0.83	0.84	0.84	0.85
44	Kuwait	0.76	0.78	0.78	–	0.81	0.83	0.84	0.84
58	Libya	–	–	–	–	–	–	0.79	0.80
71	Oman	0.49	0.55	0.64	0.70	0.73	0.76	0.77	0.78
77	Saudi Arabia	0.60	0.66	0.67	0.71	0.74	0.76	0.77	0.77
81	Lebanon	–	–	–	0.67	0.73	0.75	0.76	0.76
89	Tunisia	0.52	0.57	0.62	0.66	0.70	0.73	0.75	0.75
90	Jordan	–	0.64	0.66	0.68	0.71	0.74	0.75	0.75
94	Turkey	0.59	0.61	0.65	0.68	0.73	–	0.75	0.75
99	Iran	0.57	0.57	0.61	0.65	0.69	0.72	0.73	0.74
102	Palestinian Territories	–	–	–	–	–	–	0.73	0.73
103	Algeria	0.51	0.56	0.61	0.65	0.67	0.69	0.70	0.72
106	Syria	0.53	0.58	0.61	0.64	0.66	0.68	0.71	0.72
119	Egypt	0.43	0.49	0.54	0.58	0.61	–	0.65	0.66
124	Morocco	0.42	0.47	0.51	0.54	0.57	0.60	0.62	0.63
141	Sudan	0.34	0.37	0.39	0.42	0.47	0.49	0.51	0.51
151	Yemen	–	–	–	0.39	0.44	0.47	0.48	0.48

Source: UN, *Human Development Reports*: Arab States, 2004; 2005.

UN (out of 177 countries) to be amongst the high human development group in the world. With the exception of Israel, which has enjoyed outstanding trade, aid and military assistance from the US and European countries, the four Arab countries included in that rank are the small Gulf states of Qatar, Bahrain, UAE and Kuwait, which mostly enjoy the benefits of large oil reserves. The rest of the countries of the region, particularly those which have been involved in civil or border conflicts, have very poor human development records and lag behind most Latin American and South East Asian countries. Human development progress has been the poorest in the counties that have been engaged in prolonged military conflict. These include Syria, Jordan, Iran, Egypt and the Palestinian Territories.

The poor human development picture of the countries of the region is reflective of the overall economic and political conditions prevailing over the past three decades. Economic growth in the region, with few exceptions, has closely shadowed the boom and bust in the international oil market and the vast oil revenues earned during the boom time have not been translated into sustainable economic growth. The sparsely populated oil-exporting countries of the region have mainly 'recycled' most of their oil revenues in the West, while the relatively highly populated oil-exporting countries used their oil windfall for inflated government apparatus, lavish subsidies and high military expenditure. The decline of the oil revenues of the region during economic downturns equally brought enormous hardship to the ordinary public during the 1980s and 1990s. Since governments were unable and indeed not equipped with policies and skills to deal with the adverse effects of the boom and bust cycles, the public, and the lower classes in particular, have borne the brunt of the economic adjustment. Table 1.2 shows that the 1980s could truly be called the lost decade for the region. While global integration has been associated with accelerating growth for the East Asian countries, the table shows that per capita income growth rates in the Middle East shrunk by 1.76 per cent during the 1980s. Indeed, despite the region's positive growth rate during the 1990s, this was not sufficient to compensate for the losses of the 1980s. The economic downturn during the 1980s was so severe that the decline of per capita income in the region during the 1980s was more than twice the decline of per capita income in sub-Saharan African countries.

Table 1.3 shows the annual per capita growth of various regions of the world and the percentage of population in each per capita income growth rate band. It reveals that in the period 1990–2003, only 60 per cent of the people in Arab countries enjoyed a per capita income growth rate of more than 1 per cent, compared with 99 per cent of people in East Asia and 79 per cent of people in Latin America. On average, 13 per cent of the population of the Arab countries (34 million people) endured a shrink in their per capita income from 1990 to 2003. In this respect, the Arab countries have been the second worst-performing group of countries after the sub-Saharan African countries.

The Middle East has also been afflicted by political instability, cross-border conflict and devastating wars. There is no doubt that in addition to the destructive outcomes of the conflicts, the prolonged lack of stability has also severely reduced the region's economic and human potential. In the quest for understanding the factors that have led to the poor economic and human development in the region, this book endeavours to highlight the adverse consequences of high military spending and military conflict. The next section will briefly highlight the major causes of the major conflicts in the Middle East.

Table 1.2 Per capita income and population growth, by region, 1970–2000

Region	Population	Per capita Income[2]			Growth rates[3]					
					Population			Per capita income		
	2000[1]	1980	2000	%	1970	1980s	1990s	1970s	1980s	1990s
East Asia & Pacific	–	297	949	219.7	2.09	1.61	1.31	5.0	5.69	6.24
Latin America & Caribbean	510	3,519	3,808	8.2	2.45	2.03	1.66	3.3	–0.16	1.20
Middle East & North Africa	294	2,072	2,050	–0.01	2.59	3.13	2.35	–	–1.76	1.36
Sub-Saharan Africa	638	660	566	–0.14	2.80	2.92	2.64	–	–0.67	–0.65

Notes: 1. Millions.
2. GDP per capita income (constant 1995 US$).
3. Percentage rates.

Source: World Bank: *World Development Indicators* (April 2004).

Table 1.3 Annual GDP per capita growth rates, 1990–2003

Region	Negative	0%–1%	1%–2%	More than 2%
Arab states				
Countries	5	4	2	5
Population (m)	34	70	19	139
% of total	13	27	7	53
East Asia & Pacific				
Countries	4	1	3	13
Population (m)	3	6	81	1,814
% of total	1<	1<	4	95
Latin America & Caribbean				
Countries	4	8	9	12
Population (m)	43	74	345	79
% of total	8	14	64	15
Sub-Saharan Africa				
Countries	18	8	8	11
Population (m)	319	108	171	76
% of total	47	16	25	11
World				
Countries	41	28	32	76
Population (m)	653	450	1,081	4,030
% of total	11	7	17	65

Source: Calculated from UN, *Human Development Reports*, 2005.

The major conflicts in the region

The Arab-Israeli conflict

The first major military conflict after the collapse of the Ottoman Empire was the Arab-Israeli conflict, which commenced in 1948. Its origin lies in the 1930s when European Jews began to immigrate to Palestine in the hope of establishing the homeland promised by Balfour Declaration in 1917. The Declaration stated that the British government 'view[ed] with favour the establishment in Palestine of national home for the Jewish people'. The declaration was incorporated in the Sèvres Peace Treaty with Turkey and the mandate for Palestine in 1920. The conflict resulted in four major wars and a few other mini-wars and border skirmishes between the Arab countries and Israel; the 1948 war after the declaration of the state of Israel, the Suez Canal war, the Six-Day war of 1967, and the 1973 war. The East-West conflict during the Cold War had profound impacts on the conflict and strongly contributed to its continuation.

The conflict has had enormous effects on the political and economic development of the countries involved. Political instability has deprived the countries involved of a sense of normality and security, and war has always overshadowed their other objectives. The conflict and its continuation have provided a pretext for the armies of the countries to control and retain political power for too long. The social and human costs of the wars between the countries are immeasurable. In addition to the immediate human cost of the wars, there are now significantly more than four million Palestinian refugees who have been displaced and most are living in refugee camps scattered in neighbouring Arab countries and the Palestinian Territories.

After four major wars, in which the Arabs were badly defeated, resolving the conflict through conventional military means has reached a deadlock for both sides in the conflict. Egypt, as a leading Arab country, accepted the futility of military conflict much earlier than other countries and signed a peace treaty with Israel in 1979, effectively ending its state of war with that state completely. However, those who have been defeated may take their loss with a pinch of salt, but never accept the outcome willingly. The flaring up of the conflict every now and then and the Israelis' disproportionate response to the Palestinian reaction to the occupation of their land reflects this deep-seated feeling of hostility between the two sides. Until a comprehensive peace settlement is reached between the parties involved, the conflict remains one of the main obstacles to economic development and progress in the region.

The Kurdish problem

The issue of the Kurds, particularly in the north of Iraq, came to prominence largely after the ejection of Iraq from Kuwait in 1991 and the mass movement of Kurds to the borders of Iran and Turkey. Pressure from public opinion led to the creation of the so-called 'Safe Haven', which in Iraq was called the 'Northern No-fly Zone'. Since then, a semi-de facto Kurdish state has existed under the protection of US and UK air-cover. The origin of the problem could be traced back to the creation of modern states in the region after the collapse of the Ottoman Empire in the First World War. Great Britain and France, the two main victorious powers, neglected the Kurdish aspiration towards the creation of their own state as agreed in Treaty of Sèvres in 1920. The two countries subsequently signed the Treaty of Lausanne in 1923 in which the right of the Kurds to an independent homeland was revoked; their hoped-for state was annexed to the established countries of Turkey, Iraq and Syria.

The exact number of Kurds in the region is unknown due to the absence of reliable census information and the reluctance of the governments of the countries inhabited by Kurds to provide accurate figures. Rough estimates put the total number of Kurds at somewhere between 27 and 36 million, largely living in Turkey, Iran, Iraq and Syria. The long-term social and economic implications of the unresolved Kurdish question have long been neglected and at best underestimated by scholars and researchers. In Turkey, though sporadic local revolts and social unrests erupted throughout the 20th century, the problem came to national and international attention after 1985, when the Kurdish Workers Party (PKK) declared a war of independence. In Iraq and Iran, the Kurds continued civil unrest and armed struggle throughout the last century. All countries involved have missed a real opportunity for development by spending an enormous amount of vital and, in many cases, scarce resources on suppressing the Kurds. The extent of the human and economic costs of that approach remains to be investigated.

Gulf security

The west side of the Persian Gulf consists of six Arab countries, namely Kuwait, UAE, Bahrain, Qatar, Oman and Saudi Arabia. Together, they control 44.3 per cent of the world's proven oil reserves. This group of countries are militarily weak and incapable of defending themselves against the much more powerful and more highly populated neighbouring countries of Iraq and Iran, who have sought dominance in the region since the 1960s. The former Shah's government in Iran assumed some form of supremacy during the late 1960s and 1970s, albeit with the support of the US, and took the role of policing the Gulf until the Shah's overthrow in 1979. After that and until the invasion of Kuwait, Iraq took advantage of Iranian military weakness and assumed leadership in the region. During this period, the Gulf States were willingly or sometimes coerced into helping Iraq in its war and campaign to curb Iranian ambitions in the region. Despite the notoriety of the Iraqi regime during Saddam Hussein's era, the US and its allies supported the Iraqis during the latter's eight-year war with Iran. During this period, the Gulf countries offered Iraq huge financial resources, which helped to re-equip the Iraqi army and sustain its government at a time of downturn in the international oil market and the suspension of Iraqi oil exports. The financial support of the Gulf States, though it prolonged the war, made the region temporarily secure and curbed Iranian ambitions. Iraq's invasion of Kuwait in 1991, however, changed the Gulf's security picture and ushered in an era whereby the US took direct control over security by stationing its own marines in the region.

The presence of US forces in the region may have provided protection and guaranteed a safe route for the supply of oil from the region; the region, however, does not seem to be safer than before. The recent Iranian effort to acquire nuclear technology and the current security and political turmoil in Iraq makes the region highly volatile; indeed it is one of the most insecure regions in the world. The oil-rich Gulf States thus have every reason to worry about their security at such a time of political instability in their immediately neighbouring countries. Therefore they have sought long-term strategic alliance with the US to safeguard their security at a time when they have been spending enormous amounts of money on acquiring new military hardware from the West. Despite all this, the Gulf region remains sensitive militarily and the oil consumer countries regard its security as a matter of profound interest.

The rise of Islamic fundamentalism

After a decade of uncertainty, the ejection of Iraq from Kuwait in 1991 brought about direct US military control in the Gulf region. The US reputation in the Middle East, however, has long been undermined by its unequivocal support for Israel in the latter's conflict with the Arab countries. To make matters worse, the US's direct military intervention in Afghanistan and Iraq, removing the Taliban and Saddam Hussein regimes from power, has led to direct ideological and military clashes with Islamic extremists. Though the rise of Islamic fundamentalism in the region may also be attributed to other global causes, the US's direct military presence in the region and the continuation of the Israeli-Arab conflict have provided a breeding ground for further intensification of the ideological conflict between fundamentalist Islam and the West.

Unlike conventional military confrontations, the terrorism can not be won on the battleground. Therefore, the fight against terrorism takes a new dimension and involves other security forces, the cost of which may not be included in the calculation of military expenditure. Cross-country terrorism may also necessitate regional cooperation. Though such cooperation may lead to closer collaboration between various states of the region, the potential for using terrorism as a form of leverage by governments in the conflict should also not be overlooked. The intervention of Syria in Iraq through various terrorist groups in the aftermath of the US-led invasion in 2003 is a good example in this context.

The current picture of military expenditure in the region

As discussed earlier, military conflict has dominated much of the 20th-century political scene in the Middle East. By their nature, conflicts require and gradually encourage the establishment of strong armed forces. The creation of strong military institutions in structurally weak countries of the early 20th-century Middle East was a recipe for disaster. The colonial powers, namely Britain and France, initially created the armed forces of the Middle East in the early stages of their occupation during or immediately after the First World War, though in some cases there was no real need for a strong army as such, as Khadduri (1953) argues.

The main initial aims of Britain and France were to create armed forces in each country to, firstly, reinforce the power of the governments that they installed in those countries and, secondly, to manage and control the border conflicts that may have erupted because of the problematic nature of the artificial borders drawn when the countries were created.

The first major military conflict to arise was the Arab-Israel War of 1948. It outcome was devastating for the civilian governments of the region and for the Palestinians in particular. Most of the civilian governments of the region were largely regarded by the public as corrupt, as collaborators with foreign powers and as incapable of defending Palestine against the small, young Israeli state. The civilian governments also failed to meet the growing demand by their citizens for institutional and civil reforms. The vast majority of the people of the region lived in rural areas and agriculture was their main productive activity. The land ownership problem was rooted in the colonial era and the institutional setting of the installed governments. These governments were incapable of meeting the domestic demands of the wider public. Therefore it did not take too long for civil strife and resentment of government policy to become a major internal aspect of political life. The defeat of the Arab armies in the 1948 war also paved the way for the downfall of the civilian governments in the region.

Despite their military setbacks, the new armies were the strongest institutions in these new Arab countries. They initially championed the causes of the poor and adopted social objectives as well as promising to restore Arab honour and dignity in the war against Israel. They gradually removed civilian governments and established military dictatorships in Syria, Egypt, Iraq, Algeria, Yemen and Libya.

The military, now firmly in the political saddle, controlled and manipulated the allocation of resources, income distribution between different social strata, and the long-term institutional structural development of the societies they ruled. The Middle Eastern countries, however, were underdeveloped and largely poor in resources during the 1950s and 1960s. Therefore, the scope for high military expenditure and the growth of armies were curtailed by the lack of financial resources in this period. The two most prominent factors which led to the strengthening of the role of the armies in the region were the oil-price rise in the 1970s, which provided finance for acquiring sophisticated and expensive military hardware, and the intensification of the Cold War between the Soviet bloc and the US and its Western European allies. The rivalry between East and West provided the impetus for the continuation and intensification of conflict and the oil-price rise provided the necessary financial resources for maintaining the military establishment in government and paying for new armaments.

The small and rather weak armies established by the colonial countries became strong institutions of power and coercion thanks to a constant, intense state of war and conflict and to the windfall oil revenues received during the 1970s. They quickly became the best organised and most well-resourced institutions in Arab societies and assumed the role of 'protector of the nation' in most of them, as Halliday (2005) argues. Civilians were no longer trusted to lead the nation and civilian institutions were either fundamentally undermined or, at best, under the de facto control of the military. Laws were drafted in military barracks rather than in legal courts or democratically elected institutions.

There is no doubt that the scope for such military expansion would have been limited in the absence of the dramatic rise in the price of oil at the beginning of the 1970s. The sudden quadrupling of oil prices in 1973 created a bonanza for the various militaries. Regional military expenditure accelerated immediately to an unprecedented scale. Within one year, according to the Stockholm International Peace Research Institute (SIPRI), the value of arms transfers into the region jumped from $5.339bn in 1972 to $10.269bn in 1973 (SIPRI Yearbook 1988). According to Lebovic and Ishaq (1987), during the first period of high oil prices, 1973–82, the military expenditure of the region accounted for one-third of the military spending of all developing countries and almost one-half of world arms imports. The rise of oil revenues of the region, therefore, fuelled the conflict and lubricated the war machinery of the region.

The 1980s however, was a period of international economic downturn. Subsequently, the price of oil declined massively, which in turn led to a substantial decline in the region's oil revenues. The economies of the region therefore went into recession and standards of living deteriorated.

Therefore, despite the devastating and costly Iran-Iraq war of the 1980s, military expenditure as a percentage of GNP of the region remained relatively stable or decelerated during 1980s (Sandler and Hartley 1995; Looney 1995). In addition to the slump in the international oil market, the Egyptian-Israeli Peace Treaty in 1979 also reduced military tension and the scope for an all-out Arab war against Israel. There is no doubt that the cooling of the Cold War also contributed in the scaling down of militarisation of the region.

However, it was not too long before the region was plunged into another war with regional and international consequences. In 1991 Iraq, which had just emerged from an eight-year-long war with Iran, invaded the small city-state of Kuwait. With a small population and a small army, Kuwait was no match for the colossal Iraqi army hardened in the war with Iran. The country was overrun within few hours. The invasion plunged the whole region into a new political and military crisis. Since Kuwait and other small Gulf States own large oil reserves, there was too much at stake for the US and the European countries. The invasion suddenly put Iraq at the helm of the Gulf security and potentially threatened the oil-rich Kingdom of Saudi Arabia as well as the other small Gulf States. Therefore the US took upon itself the responsibility of evicting Iraq from Kuwait.

Iraq's subsequent swift removal from Kuwait had long-lasting effects on the region's long-term security and stability, with the US military action bringing its forces into the region on a semi-permanent basis.

Table 1.4 shows the world and regional military expenditure between 1988 and 2007. The data show that military expenditure in the Middle East has been on an increasing trend with the exception of a

Table 1.4 World and regional military expenditure in $bn at constant 2005 prices and exchange rate, 1988–2007

Region	**1988**	**1990**	**1995**	**2000**	**2005**	**2006**	**2007**	**% change 1988–2007**
Africa	12.1	12.5	10.7	12.3	16.0	15.8	16.8	+38.8
USA	525	493	397	382	548	559	598	+14.0
Asia & Oceania	102	110	124	139	176	186	200	+96.1
Europe	514	468	283	287	306	311	319	−38.0
Middle East	41.1	53.0	40.8	54.3	67.2	73.9	79.0	+92.2
World	1195	1136	855	875	1113	1145	1214	+1.5
Change from previous year (%)	–	−3.3	−4.8	+3.8	+4.0	+2.9	+6.0	–

Source: SIPRI, *Yearbook* (2008).

decline in the first half of the 1990s. SIPRI data show that the region's military expenditure started to decline immediately after the First Gulf War. This reduction coincides with the collapse of the Soviet bloc which subsequently led to loss of the region's traditional arms suppliers. The eviction of Iraq from Kuwait, which led to the Western economic and military boycotting of that country, reduced and eventually eliminated Iraq's capacity to replenish its lost military hardware and reduced its military expenditure significantly. However, as the data show, regional military expenditure started to increase gradually from the last part of the 1990s, reaching $54.3bn by 2000. The total expenditure increased further to $67.1bn by 2005 and reached $79bn in 2007. The percentage increase from 1988 to 2007 amounts to a record 92 per cent. The only other region that matched such an unprecedented rise was Asia and Oceania and the increase came in a period when world military expenditure grew by only 1.5 per cent.

Given this picture, it is not surprising that SIPRI data on the volume of major conventional weapons trade shows that among the 15 highest recipient countries of arms, six Middle Eastern countries rank prominently. Turkey is ranked 5th, Egypt 6th, UAE 8th, Iran 11th, Israel 13th and Saudi Arabia 15th (SIPRI 2005). While Saudi Arabia and UAE are oil-rich countries and can easily afford expensive arms and large spending on their military and security forces, and Israel's arms deals are supported by continuous US military assistance, the other three high-spending countries, namely Iran, Egypt and Turkey, have different socio-political circumstances. These three countries have large populations and their per capita incomes are a fraction of those of the other high-spending countries. Therefore, although Egypt and Turkey receive some military assistance from the US, the sustainability of high military expenditure in all these countries must come at the expense of other public expenditure vital for the wellbeing of their large populations.

The analytical framework of this book

The Middle East has long been facing a multi-faceted economic and political dilemma. Economic stagnation and gloomy prospects for development are the consequence of long-term historical, cultural and structural factors. Historically speaking, the establishment of the modern states in the region was largely based on the interests of the colonial powers at the end of the First World War. In order to manage the newly formed countries and in the absence of modern social and civil institutions in them, the colonial powers had to either draw support from the remnants of the institutions left behind by the Ottoman Empire or to resort to the old tribal system dominant in the region. It is worth mentioning that the colonial powers did not consider holding referendums or democratic elections as a viable alternative. The first two choices were inherently problematic; firstly, the remnants of the Ottoman institutions were undemocratic and based on rules and regulations that were not fit for governing modern countries. Nevertheless, the best sources of skills were mainly to be found in the institutions that the old Ottoman Empire left behind. Consequently, army officers had a strong presence in the newly formed government institutions and the armies that were created after independence became the best organised institutions in the new societies. It comes as no surprise, then, that after a relatively short period of time the armies took power in most countries of the region.

The second option, which still plagues the region, was tantamount to keeping the region backwardly oriented. There is no doubt that the old traditions, whether based in ethnic cultures or in religion, did not conform to the values and ethics of modernity and hence stood against developmental aspirations. Therefore, the colonial powers resorted to a combination of both choices, as neither was capable of exclusively providing the foundation for running a state. They revitalised Ottoman civil institutions and established relatively strong armies under the leadership of officers from the Ottoman army. This left a long-lasting legacy for future governance and distribution of wealth in the region. The role of the armed forces and high military expenditure is therefore structurally inherited from the original formation of the countries of the region after the First World War.

The above analysis leads us to the conclusion, as Halliday (2005) argues, that it is not the future of the Middle East, but its past, that poses the greatest challenge. To sum up, the nature of the major conflicts in the region, the internal class and power structures of societies, and the foreign powers' influence in the region, particularly during the Cold War era, have all created a socio-political environment conducive to the perpetuation of instability, the consequent militarisation of the region and high military expenditure.

The survival of old tribal and cultural relationships in the region over the past century is not due to the resilience of religion or the strength of local cultures *vis-à-vis* modernisation but largely due to the failure of other, secular, modes of governance. For instance, in Egypt, Syria, Libya, Iraq and Algeria various forms of so-called socialist governments came to power and subsequently mismanaged the economy and hindered economic and social development, eventually creating a political and ideological vacuum that was inevitably filled by the revival of Islamic tendencies, mostly with a hint of extremism.

Given the complex socio-political background of the region, it would be highly simplistic and intellectually misleading to treat military expenditure and the role of the military in the region as resulting from simple demand-and-supply market activity. This book will therefore attempt to adopt a political economy framework of analysis. It will look at the military's role in the governments of the region, their rise to power and their influence on the shaping of the socio-political development of various countries. Each chapter will first investigate the origin of the military in a country and discuss its gradual development and rise to power. In each case, a brief discussion of the justification for high military expenditure will be carried out in the context of perceived internal and external threats to the country. Each chapter will also analyse, though briefly, the economic development and economic growth of the country since 1970 and highlight its weaknesses and potential strengths. Military expenditure will be discussed in each decade since the 1970s, ending in 2006. Conclusions will be made at the end of each chapter.

The choice of the countries for investigation was consciously made to relate to the major endemic conflicts mentioned in the second part of this chapter. Therefore, Iran and Iraq have been chosen largely because of their influence and role in Gulf security and its military balance. Both countries have also inherited the Kurdish problem, which has become a major domestic military and security issue. Turkey has been chosen largely because of its history and its relationship to the Kurdish problem, one that it is still far from resolving satisfactorily. The other three countries, namely Syria, Egypt and Israel, are major players in the Arab-Israeli conflict and their roles in regional socio-political development have been paramount. This book, however, does not cover the military role and (quite significant) military expenditure of the Gulf States, largely because of their insignificant impact on the military balance of the region.

The next chapter will provide an in-depth review the literature on military expenditure and its effects on the economy, from Adam Smith until the present, highlighting the main controversies in the area. The following chapters will investigate the main participating countries in the major conflicts highlighted by this chapter – Iran, Turkey, Iraq, Syria, Egypt and Israel.

The multidisciplinary nature of the investigation of this book, however, does not make it a substitute for separate studies of each aspect of the socio-political nature of the region. Each such aspect merits separate, detailed study which is beyond the scope of this book. The aim of this book remains modest in offering a reasonably balanced view of the role and economic costs of the military and military conflict in the region.

2
The Economics of Military Expenditure: A Literature Review

Military expenditure and its measurement problems

Since ancient times, man has shaped its existence and surroundings by the use of force more than anything else. Indeed, the use of collective force in the form of military activity has been regarded as necessary for the protection of established civilisations as well as for expanding the boundary of existing ones. The epic journeys of warriors in ancient Babylon, ancient Greece and the Roman Empire, Islamic conquerors and the Mongols were all based on warriors seeking to defeat the enemy or to acquire and rule new territories under various pretexts.

Amassing a relatively huge force at any time requires the removal of men and equally animals, tools and *matériel* from productive and civil activities to be used for the preparation of and actual execution of warfare. This action has had a double-edged effect on societies. Firstly, spare time was required for soldiers to train and prepare for war and to be away from the production of goods and services intended for civilian consumption for a long period of time. The opportunity cost of the absence of men from productive sectors of the economy leads to the loss of output that they would have produced for themselves and others in the absence of their engagement in military operations. The loss of production would exert an extra burden on the remaining labour force in civilian production and in many cases this would lead to starvation of the civilian population, as food surplus usually would be expropriated by warring armies during prolonged wars. Secondly, the men involved in wars the preparation for war would require feeding, clothing and equipment. Most of these would have to be produced by others. This would have two important, albeit not exclusive, effects on the society. On the one hand, extra taxes in the form of money or produce would have to be imposed and collected prior and during wars. This would obviously reduce the financial ability of the civilian population to spend money as their disposable income would decrease and on the other hand, some civilian manufacturing would have to be geared towards producing specific warfare-related products, such as swords, shields, bombs, tanks and the like. Even ignoring the destructive consequences of war itself, the conversion of civilian productive activities into military activities exerts a huge burden on the civil society.

Military expenditure data related to national defence activities are usually set out in governments' fiscal reports but these do not include the opportunity costs mentioned above. Researchers, however, define the ratio of military expenditure to the gross national product of a country as the 'military burden'. There are however, two important clarifications that have to be made to make sense out of such data. The first is: What constitutes 'military expenditure'?

The definition of military expenditure (milex hereafter) varies from one organisation to another. The four prominent international agencies that have collected and reported data on military expenditure are the International Monetary Fund (IMF), the International Institute for Strategic Studies (IISS), the US Arms Control and Disarmament Agency (ACDA), and the Stockholm International Peace Research Institute (SIPRI). As Ball (1987) states, ACDA and SIPRI have definitions that are based on the NATO definition of milex, with slight differences. Both agencies are now making an effort to bring the data they collect into conformity with each other. The NATO definition describes milex as covering:

> All current and capital expenditure on the armed forces, in the running of defence departments and other government agencies engaged in defence projects as well as space projects; the costs of paramilitary forces and police when judged to be trained and equipped for military operation; military R&D, tests and evaluation costs; and the costs of retirement pensions of civilian employees, military aid are concluded in the expenditure of the donor countries. Excluded are items on civilian defence, interest on war debts and veterans' payments (Sen 1992: p. 172).

The main difference between the ACDA and SIPRI definitions is that ACDA excludes expenditure on internal security while SIPRI includes it. The important difference between the NATO and IMF definitions is in the area of foreign military aid. Since the IMF data is in principle based on national account practices, reporting data on milex data may or may not include foreign military aid. For the same reason, the burden of military pensions is borne by the civilian sector. ACDA and SIPRI are revising their earlier estimates of milex by substantial amounts. This makes statistical analysis and inferences based on currently published data highly unreliable. It is also important to mention that ACDA data does not come from an independent data source. ACDA data is extracted from official trade statistics on military transfers compiled by the US Departments of State and Defense. For data on foreign countries, ACDA uses official US government sources. This basically implies that ACDA data is neither independently collected nor impartially processed. It comes from US government sources and it is therefore very difficult to verify the accuracy and validity of data complied by this institution.

SIPRI data collection has also encountered fundamental problems. The collection of data is based on governments' reporting of their milex to SIPRI, the UN and NATO. Table 2.1 shows the number of countries covered by the three organisations which request data on milex from countries. In total, about 21 per cent of the countries covered in the SIPRI milex coverage reported data during 2000. With the exception of the NATO, South American and Central European countries, the rate of reply to questionnaires of other groups of countries is also very poor.

Table 2.1 Response rates to military expenditure questionnaires, 2000

Region	SIPRI coverage	SIPRI request	SIPRI replies	NATO replies	UN coverage	UN replies	Total replies
Africa	50	50	6	–	52	1	7
N. America	2	0	0	2	2	2	2
C. America	8	13	2	–	13	1	2
S. America	11	11	5	–	12	3	7
C. Asia	5	5	0	–	5	1	1
E. Asia	16	16	2	–	16	1	3
S. Asia	6	6	2	–	6	1	2
Oceania	4	3	1	–	6	1	1
W. Europe	20	7	1	13	20	11	20
C./E. Europe	15	15	5	3	15	8	11
Europe, CSI	7	7	10	–	7	1	1
Middle East	15	13	2	1	15	1	3
Small states	–	–	–	–	20	–	–
Total	159	146	34	19	189	32	60

Note: Figures refer to number of countries.
Source: Sköns (2002).

In the Middle East, only Jordan, Lebanon and Turkey have reported their military expenditure.

Having an appropriate definition of milex, as Sen (1992) argues, does not guarantee strict adherence to it. The international organisations that report and process milex data rely heavily on national governments as the main source of their data. Understating or misreporting spending on military forces, particularly in developing countries, is quite common for a variety of reasons. Firstly, the size and the fighting capability of armed forces are regarded sensitive by governments. Therefore, they are shrouded in secrecy. Developing countries' governments are reluctant to release and disseminate full information about their armies to neighbouring countries in order to prevent arms races. Since many developing countries are relatively recently created, they are in constant border disputes with their neighbours, and some are actually at war or under the threat of hostilities from neighbouring countries. At best, neighbouring countries are regarded as potential enemies, and therefore, not revealing the extent of military expenditure and the fighting capability of a country's armed forces is regarded to be in the best interests of the security of the country.

Secondly, governments are mostly reluctant to release full information about milex to their own citizens. Many developing countries suffer from prolonged domestic political and social instability, and control over the public in a wider sense has been a preoccupation of governments in many developing countries. It is also worth mentioning that the military elites in developing countries are the most privileged and best-paid social strata in society. The military elite, therefore, protects its socio-economic interests by limiting the release of milex information and data to the public. This problem is not confined to developing countries only. Blocking access to sensitive information or data on various aspects of milex can also be even observed in many developed countries. Examples include the UK's expenditure of £1.1bn on Chevaline, the multiple warhead developed by Britain for her Polaris missiles, which was concealed from the public during the early 1980s (Neild 1981), the concealment of UK government aid to Saddam Hussein's regime in the aftermath of the chemical bombardment of the town of Halabja in 1988 (revealed by the Scott inquiry in 1996), and the Bush administration's designation of some information about the historical total of Minuteman, Titan and other missiles as security secrets (Lee 2006).

Thirdly, the collection of milex data in developing countries suffers from fundamental statistical problems; developing countries lack the necessary trained experts, organisational structure and adequate funds to collect and disseminate data on various aspects of their milex. Hence, the quality of milex data in developing countries varies from one country to another. This renders comparison between developing countries' defence spending highly problematic.

The milex data published by international agencies is also tainted with inconsistency; firstly, milex data published by the main agencies is converted into the US dollar using different conversion methods. For instance, in order to produce consistent data, different agencies use different inflators. The Stockholm International Peace Research Institute (SIPRI) uses the consumer price index while the US Arms Control and Disarmament Agency (ACDA) uses the GNP price index. The two agencies also frequently express data for the same period using different base years. This makes comparison across sources for researchers almost impossible. Table 2.2 shows that even if agencies use similar base years, their data may diverge by tens of billions of US dollars. It is also important to note that agencies tend to revise the previously published data, and the difference between the revised and already published data could amount to billions of dollars. For instance, in 2006, SIPRI revised data on Middle East milex during 2004 and the difference with the 2005 published data is $2.8 billion. Therefore, researchers may unwittingly infer different analytical and policy recommendations from different sources of data.

Conversion of local currency data into US dollars brings about yet another measurement problem. Since there is a relatively large divergence between the purchasing power parity (PPP) and the market value of a currency, milex data in US dollars may not reflect the true costs of milex to a developing country. For instance, the economic burden of a per-capita spending of $100 in a poor African country is far greater than the same per-capita spending in an oil-producing country. Therefore, to assess the true economic burden of milex, economists agree that data

Table 2.2 Middle East ACDA and SIPRI milex data in $bn, 1992–9

Year	(1) ACDA[1]	(2) SIPRI[2]	(1)–(2)
1992	93	52.3	+40.7
1993	58	51.0	+7.0
1994	53	50.9	+2.1
1995	52	47.9	+4.1
1996	56	48.9	+7.1
1997	57	53.5	+3.5
1998	54	57.8	−3.8
1999	55	56.1	−1.1

Notes: 1. ACDA data is in constant 1999 dollars.
2. SIPRI data is in constant 1998 prices.
Sources: WMEAT (2003), SIPRI, *Yearbook* (2002).

in national currencies better reflects the real costs of milex than the data converted into a common currency. To overcome this problem, PPP milex data has to be constructed for every country. To do so, the PPP costs for the best alternative use of the resource used by the military has to be calculated. Though efforts have been made by international agencies to overcome this difficulty by using milex PPP, public expenditure PPP and GNP PPP, the problem is far from having been resolved satisfactorily (see Brzoska 1981).

The second problem is that developing countries do not uniformly and consistently follow a well-specified method of data calculation or definition of milex. For instance, some countries may include part of their milex data under the budget of other ministries. Good examples in this respect are military pensions, and debt incurred through the procurement of armaments. On the other hand, civilian expenditure may be recorded as defence spending. For instance, Pakistan and Saudi Arabia include civil aviation spending in their milex data.

The conclusion to be drawn from the above is that national governments are the main sources of errors and omissions in milex data. They tend to include or exclude various parts of milex in their calculation either deliberately to mislead their neighbouring countries and their own citizens or otherwise they simply lack the expertise, organisational capabilities and resources essential to the calculation of data in general. The severity of the problem limits the validity of the inferences that researchers can deduce from using these figures. For the same reason and in most cases, cross-country comparison is ineffective. The widespread doubts about the accuracy of published data also shed grave doubts on the soundness of the statistical analysis that has proliferated in research and publications on the impacts of milex on economic growth and welfare in the past quarter of a century. As Sköns (2002) argues, official data on defence budgets and expenditures are a rather poor indicator of what the actual costs of milex are. The only statement which can be safely made about the milex data of developing countries, as Blackaby and Ohlson (1987) argue, is that it is an 'order of magnitude' statement. At best, data on milex should be treated as an indicator of military opportunity costs.

Literature review on the relationship between military expenditure and economic growth

Investigating the costs and benefits of having a standing army in times of peace as well as during periods of war has never constituted an academic discipline on its own. The study of the costs of defence expenditure has acquired prominence particularly since the publication of the seminal study by Benoit (1973). This investigated the relationship between economic growth, investment, foreign aid and certain other variables of 44 developing countries between 1950 and 1960. The method employed in this study was correlation analysis. Contrary to expectation, the research found that countries with a heavy defence expenditure burden generally had the most rapid growth rate and those with the lowest defence expenditure burden tended to have the lowest growth rates. Since then, the art of econometric model building in the area of defence expenditure has become a significant technique for researchers and practitioners. Hence, literature on the effects of milex on economic growth and welfare has flourished using similar methods of analysis, either supporting Benoit's conclusion or otherwise producing evidence to the contrary, that an increasing military burden inhibits economic growth.

The use of statistical analysis, though it may be very useful as a tool of analysis, is highly controversial in the social sciences, particularly in the study of defence economics. Defence spending is the monopoly of the state and one of its most important functions. With the exception of a few small countries, every country in the world has a standing army. Maintaining and developing the army and other military bodies absorbs a substantial part of the annual budget of governments. Policy making regarding the size, the arming and the maintenance of the military forms a crucial part of government's decision making.

The necessity of having a standing army in the modern sense goes far beyond simple economic justification. Hence, defence expenditure economics presents a far more complicated task than simple calculations of the immediate costs involved. It was Adam Smith (1776) who first drew the attention to the necessity of having a standing army in the modern world in *The Wealth of Nations*. He argued that defending society from the violence and invasion of other independent societies is 'the first duty of the sovereign', and this 'can be performed only by means of a military force'. Unlike in pre-capitalist societies, the expenses of both preparing this military force in times of peace, and of employing it in times of war, have become complex due to two important causes; 'the progress of manufacturing and the improvement of the art of war'. Until the invention of firearms and modern weaponry, arrows, catapults, shields and swords could easily be picked up and reused. However, the progress of modern weaponry has made the art of war one of the most expensive functions of a society. Smith argues that: 'The cannon and the mortar are, not only much dearer, but much heavier machines than the *ballista* or *catapulta*, and require a greater expence [sic], not only to prepare them for the field, but to carry them to it' (Smith 1976, Book V, Part 1). Therefore, the progress of technology has inevitably made war very expensive.

Adam Smith also thought about the labour input of modern warfare. He argued that in ancient times, shepherds and farmers had a great deal of leisure time and if they were involved in skirmishes and short wars, their production of food would not suffer appreciably. In their short absence, nature would continue producing their food for them. In a modern society, a worker or manufacturer has less leisure time and if he was disengaged from his profession for any length of time, nature would not produce anything on its own and he would therefore lose the produce of his labour. Therefore, in being detached from his commodity-producing profession and becoming involved in this rather 'peculiar occupation' of war, the worker or manufacturer would lose his subsistence. The complexity of modern warfare also requires some division of labour. Preparing for war during peacetime and being on standby for going into war is no longer a temporary disruption. In his justification for the necessity of a standing army, Adam Smith argued that for the provision of such an army, a certain class of society had to make the military profession their sole occupation during times of war as well as in peace, and society would have to bear the cost of their subsistence.

On the issue of the expenses of war, Smith discussed the ineffectiveness of raising taxes as a means of meeting the immediate needs of an army. He argues that increasing taxes when a war begins or the moment at which it appears to begin 'will not begin to come into the treasury till perhaps ten or twelve months after they are imposed' (Smith 1976, p. 909). The immediate increase in the financial requirement of the army at the crucial time of an imminent war 'will not wait for the gradual and slow returns of the new taxes'. In addition to this, Smith argued that modern governments are unwilling to increase taxes during the time of war 'for fear of offending the people, who, by so great and so sudden an increase of taxes, would soon be disgusted with the war', therefore, 'the facility of borrowing delivers them from the embarrassment which this fear and inability would otherwise occasion' (p. 919). Smith, therefore, concludes that 'In this exigency government can have no other resource but in borrowing' (p. 909).

Therefore, in funding wars, Adam Smith prefers borrowing to direct taxation mainly because, as mentioned above, taxes trickle down slowly and the sudden high requirements of military effort cannot wait for future payments. During periods of war, raising taxes is also an undesirable public policy. Therefore, borrowing is the more attractive option for politicians. The other reason that Smith cites for borrowing is that governments would be unable to determine the exact level of taxation required to cover a war effort. Therefore, the ease of borrowing would save them embarrassment. During prolonged wars, Adam Smith didn't rule out a moderate increase of taxes, to raise from year to year, sufficient for carrying on wars to their conclusion. Smith was also fully aware of the limitation of raising new taxes during a time when the nation is already overburdened with taxes. During such a period 'nothing but the necessities of new war, nothing but either the animosity of national vengeance, or the anxiety of national security, can induce the people to submit, with tolerable patience, to a new tax' (p. 921).

For Smith, the economic effects of allocation of resources to war efforts are manifested in his distinguishing between productive and unproductive labour. The allocation of labour and capital to war, though providing peace necessary for the progress of the society, is largely unproductive in economic terms. The allocation of capital to war efforts, borrowed or otherwise raised in the form of taxation, is 'defrayed by the annual destruction of some capital which had before existed in the country' (p. 925). War, therefore, impedes the accumulation of capital and people become more wary of its burden and causes as it continues. It is because of this reason that war prevents leaders from wantonly declaring it.

It was David Ricardo who regarded wars or the preparation for wars as a source of distress to the economy of a nation. In his 'The Principles of Political Economy and Taxation' (1817), he argued that 'The commencement of war after a long peace, or of peace after a long war, generally produces considerable distress in trade' (1992, Ch. XIX). Wars and indeed peace after prolonged wars tend to change the nature of employment of both labour and capital. During war, some labour and capital will be devoted to the production of weaponry as well as the provision of subsistence for those who are engaged in the war effort. Therefore, some labour and capital will necessarily be removed for the production of other commodities which the society has naturally produced during peacetime conditions. Wars also disrupt the pattern of trade between nations. This will inevitably change the comparative advantage of a nation. In this context, Ricardo mentions the disruption of corn imports during the time of war and how the nation must allocate some of its labour and capital to the production of the commodity in which it doesn't have a comparative advantage. At the end of a war and the return of normal conditions of trade, the nation will not be able to produce the expensive corn produced during wartime as such production is not competitive and imported corn from foreign countries is cheaper. This will exert sudden and harmful distress on the economy of the country. Labour that was employed in the production of expensive corn during a war will become unemployed and the capital devoted to the production of corn will become redundant. Wars are also harmful to exporting countries of corn in that they suddenly interrupt both production and trade. Exports of corn will be halted and the labour and capital which were devoted to the production of corn will suddenly become redundant.

Ricardo, unlike Adam Smith, who regarded a standing army as a prerequisite for peace and prosperity of modern nations, considered war as the product of the 'absurd jealousies' that prevail between different nations. War impairs the allocation of resources as it distorts the pattern of trade of certain goods and makes the production of some goods necessary during the time of war, and the harmful effects of war will last much longer than the actual war itself. It takes nations years to overcome the adverse effects of war and readjust to the normal conditions of production and free trade. Financing war efforts can also spill over into the future. War can be either financed by taxes or loans. Self-promoting politicians who would rather not antagonise the public by increasing taxation during a war would prefer to finance wars by loans, shifting the burden of the costs of war into the future. However, if war is financed by taxation, the burden of the war will be on the present generation and will be felt by the public immediately. In a democratic country, the government may be faced by public opposition to war. Ricardo argued that 'When the pressure of the war is felt at once, without mitigation, we shall be less disposed wantonly to engage in an expensive contest, and if engaged in it, we shall be sooner disposed to get out of it unless it was a contest of some great national interest' (Ricardo 1951 [1820], p. 186).

Unfortunately many countries go into war without proper public debate about its causes and consequences and therefore, politicians are less restrained than Ricardo imagines. It is also true that there are important national issues that should not be left to the simple calculation of taxes when nations are faced with threats to their liberty, but it is equally true that if politicians are left free, they would justify a war for a strip of uninhabited and worthless land.

David Ricardo, in general, regarded war as a 'retrograde' activity that temporarily arrests the progress of society and causes unnecessary suffering to both people and the economy. In this Ricardo remained true to his principle of comparative advantage of trade and his unconditional support for free trade between nations.

Thomas Malthus, in his 'Essay on the Principle of Population' (1798) regarded war as a preventative and positive check on population growth. He argued that 'population, when unchecked, increased in a geometrical ratio, and subsistence for man in a arithmetical ration' (Malthus 2004 [1798], p. 15). The assumption was that under the condition of equality and abundant food, the rate of population growth would be much greater than the rate of growth of food supplies. Therefore, if population is not checked by the 'preventative and the positive checks' such as 'vicious customs with respect to women, great cities, unwholesome manufactures, luxury, pestilence, and war' (p. 45), overpopulation will eventually be brought to a halt by the lack of proper and sufficient food for a further increase.

Malthus's theory of population increase is mainly based on two main assumptions. Firstly, constant return to scale whereby the growth of subsistence is determined and influenced by the limitation of nature. As the population increases, and as the supply of fertile and arable land is fixed by nature, more labour will be working on the same piece of land and the law of diminishing returns will obtain in the production process and the marginal contribution of food production by extra labour will decline gradually. Modern development of food production processes has proven this simplistic assumption wrong. The application of modern science in the fields of land fertility, seed selection, genetic engineering, the development of disease-resistant species of plants and animals, and the application of advanced technology has proved the assumption unfounded. The increasing return to scale of modern farming has increased the production of food beyond the limits of the population needs of the world. Indeed, the main problem of the market for agricultural products nowadays is a glut of commodities rather than a shortage of food. If starvation is experienced anywhere, then its causes can be found in the manner in which the social system allocates resources. There is no doubt that even in the face of severe droughts experienced by sub-Saharan African countries, the world is still capable of producing enough food to eradicate starvation and prevent famine.

The other assumption of the Malthusian theory of population is the positive correlation between population growth and per capita income. Malthus believed that as living conditions, particularly of the lower classes, improved, the fertility rate would tend to be higher than the mortality rate and overpopulation would be inevitable. As Michael Todaro (2000) argues, research on developing countries indicates that there is no clear correlation between population growth rates and levels of per capita income. In conclusion, Malthus, therefore, was mainly concerned with the impact of war on population growth rather than with its costs and consequences.

Karl Marx did not write about the economics of milex or the economics of war *per se* but looked at war from the standpoint of conventional morality and from a historical-dialectic point of view. Marx hoped that Prussia would win the 1870 war against France largely because of his understanding of the outcome of that war. In his analysis, the war would lead to the unification of Germany and a more centralised working-class movement (Mehring 1962, p. 438). His public view, which was formulated for addressing the General Council of Workers, rested upon the idea of justice and common morality. In his recommendation for workers during the Franco-Prussian war, he, on behalf of the General Council, advised German workers to 'accept the war as a necessary evil' (Marx and Engels 1951, Vol. I, p. 441). He justified this position by his understanding of the nature of the war from the standpoint of who was the victim and who was the aggressor. Since France was the aggressor, German workers, by the nature of class struggle, were not expected to fight their French comrades, but they had to accept the war because it has been imposed on their country. They were therefore recommended to fight a defensive war. In other words, according to Marx, German workers should only fight within internationally recognised borders. French workers, on the contrary, were called upon to oppose the war and overthrow their government.

Though the full Marxist analysis of the effects of military expenditure on capital accumulation or capital destruction, that is, surplus-producing or surplus-consuming, is beyond the scope of this study, the traditional Marxist analysis of military expenditure and its effects on the development of capitalism was largely developed by 20th-century Marxist scholars such as Paul Baran and Paul Sweezy. To be fair, the idea that excessive military expenditure is promoted to ease the stagnation experienced by capitalism was originally discussed by Marx's collaborator Friedrich Engels. Engels saw two distinctive characteristics of expensive military expenditure for European nations during the latter half of the 19th century. He first regarded expensive and costly military hardware as 'outrageously costly' and a 'lavish waste of money' (Engels 1975, pp. 207–8). This understanding of high military expenditure forms the basis for the analyses of later Marxist theorists who argue that high military spending is a mechanism to save capitalism from permanent stagnation and who regard it as the main means of prolonging the life of capitalism. The other effect of high military spending, according to Engels, is that the excessive financial burden required for sophisticated military hardware and aggressive competition between European countries in building strong and well-equipped armies was expected to hasten 'their financial collapse' (p. 204). The rise of militarism in Europe during the last half of the 19th century and the increasing reliance on universal compulsory military service would, in Engels's view, transform the armies of princes and principalities into armies of people. He eventually anticipated that the military machine of governments would 'refuse to serve the rulers and [that] militarism [would] collapse by the dialectics of its own evolution' (pp. 204–5).

There is no doubt that although the global rise of military expenditure burden has became an important theoretical and moral issue widely discussed and analysed by modern Marxist and non-Marxist economists, the people's army envisaged by Engels didn't materialise beyond the first quarter of the 20th century. While in Germany and Russia the mass conscripts exhausted by the prolonged and devastating First World War became sympathetic to workers' revolution, European armies never had any substantial or systematic inclination towards a revolutionary change or had any revolutionary effect on the working-class movement. In contrast, the idea of the people's army dominated the political scenery of many developing countries in the postcolonial era with devastating consequences for the social and economic potentials of those countries. In many developing countries, the army, under the pretext of defending and protecting the national interest and claiming to be the true representative of the people, took executive and legislative powers into their hands and to a large extent squandered the scarce resources of those countries during crucial periods of their development.

Jean-Baptiste Say is perhaps the first classical economist who took the analysis of military expenditure beyond the simple costs of military hardware. In his *Treatise of Political Economy* (1821), he introduced the importance of the human costs of military action and the economic destruction that war causes. In his discussion of whether a standing army is a necessity for modern societies, he argued that 'it would be an immense inconvenience if every citizen were liable to be dragged from a productive employment, which has become necessary to society for the purposes of national defence' (Say 1821, Vol. II, Book III, Chap. VI, p. 304). Since it would be highly disruptive for landowners, manufacturers and traders to leave their regular occupation and sacrifice their time and talent to join the army, it would be more convenient for them to pay taxes 'that may enable the monarch or the republic to defend the country against external violence with a hired and professional soldiery, who are, however, too apt to become the tools of their leader's ambition or tyranny' (p. 305). Modern warfare, in Say's opinion, requires the extensive application of science and a division of labour. The productive labourer engaged in subsistence and adding extra value to the general stock of wealth of the nation would be disengaged from this normal economic activity and become a hired professional soldier. This professional soldier 'not only adds no product of his own to the general stock of wealth, in return for the necessary subsistence he consumes, but is often set to work to destroy the fruits of other people's labour and toil' (p. 309). Soldiers are not just consuming but destroying the fruits of labour of others, therefore 'war costs a nation more than its expenses' (p. 308). In this regard, Say is close to Engels and to later Marxist economists who considered armies as unproductive and destructive political institutions in the hand of warmongers and tyrants.

Ignoring the immense costs of military industries at this stage, the opportunity cost of soldiers being away from their productive activities is the loss of their produce and the consumption of goods produced by other labourers. In addition to the fact that soldiers are completely unproductive, they are also destructive. Unfortunately, the modern economics of milex, which has been relegated to the art of model building and mechanical quantitative analysis, has not just neglected the full opportunity cost of modern military machinery but ignored the devastating consequences of its activities.

Though wars before the First World War were destructive by any measure, they were never as destructive as or had the wide-reaching effects of the First World War. At the end of the last quarter of the 19th century, the scale of wars was transformed by the expansion of colonialism among European nations and the scramble to divide Africa. The competition between these countries, particularly between Great Britain, Germany and France for a bigger share of the world, required massive and sophisticated naval and merchant fleets. This was perhaps the second biggest shift in milex after the advent of gunpowder. In 1898, the standing armies of the European countries stood at 3,562,000 men, one million more than in 1858. The cost of the naval powers was equivalent to or greater than the costs of the standing armies. The colossal costs of armies led the Tsar of Russia to call for a reduction of economic burdens imposed on the European nations by excessively large armies. This first attempt at global disarmament led to the Hague Conference on January 1899. The Russian initiative was met with considerable resistance from Great Britain, the US and Germany and its failure led to a further expansion of the European armies.

The third stage in the growth of milex was due to the invention of air power and the massive production of armaments just before the outbreak of the First World War. Indeed, as Kennedy (1975) argues, the First World War created a cast-iron connection between military power and the industrial system. War no longer depended on military formation or the bravery and dexterity of men but rather on the capacity of the country's industrial sector to produce and sustain armament production at a scale required for global total war.

F. W. Hirst, a liberal English journalist who was the editor of the *Economist* at the beginning of the 20th century, became alarmed by the enormous costs of war preparation and later the scale of the war. He published his *The Political Economy of War* in 1915. In the tradition of Ricardo, Say and Engels rather than Adam Smith, he was suspicious of the European rulers and fiercely against 'the menace of armament' (Hirst 1915, p. 97). He argued that 'although it is clearly the interest of mankind to make proportional reductions of armaments, the groups that manage mankind have preferred to arrange a competitive race, which is bound to end in general disaster' (p. 95). He strongly argued that the wealth of Europe was no longer threatened with annihilation by barbarous poverty; rather the danger was that 'civilised nations will ruin one another by applying their wealth to the machinery of destruction' (p. 11).

In his argument against the growing war machinery in Europe, Hirst listed three fallacies of proponents of high military expenditure. The first was that war increases wealth by circulating money; the second was it increases wealth by creating a demand for the things that it has destroyed; the third was that it increases wealth by reducing unemployment. The first fallacy, in Hirst's view, stems from a confusion between wealth and money. To finance war, governments resort to printing paper money. This debases the currency, raises prices and wages and leads to the country eventually abandoning its support of a stable exchange rate for its currency. All this will inevitably lead to 'a general decline in the standard of civilised life'. He cited that the warring nations of Europe, except Great Britain, immediately abandoned the gold standard. Hirst regards the second fallacy as being as absurd as the first. Though there would be an attempt by the survivors of the war to rebuild what war has destroyed, not everything will be able to be restored to its pre-war condition and the extent of the rebuilding would depend on the ability of the survivors and the capacity of the economy to restore and rebuild. On the third fallacy, Hirst, in line with his predecessors, argues that 'war diverts employment from productive to destructive arts. It enormously reduces employment in peace industries and enormously increases it in war industries' (p. 124). Hirst also acknowledges that war does benefit a minority but ultimately at the expense of the general public, who bear the cost of war and mourn those who perish in war. He argued that 'we are in no way concerned to deny that many individual traders, shipowners, financiers may and do make fortunes out of war ... In times of war able and respectable men of business may become bankrupts while worthless favourites and corrupt contractors make money quickly' (p. 125).

The concern over the consequences of war and war machinery are equally shared by A. C. Pigou who wrote about the political economy of war after the First World War. In the *Political Economy of War*, published in 1921, he accepted a standing army as a precautionary measure against the menaces of possible war itself. In this, Pigou's argument is not dissimilar to Adam Smith's justification for having a standing army to protect the wealth of a civilised nation against the threats of barbarians. Pigou, however, goes further than that by arguing that the standing army and the constant requirement for competitive armament will inevitably lead to the development of an armament industry. The peculiar nature of this industry is evident from the fact that it goes beyond the rhetoric of necessity of national defence. In an effort to sell their deadly products, armament firms 'promote war scares and international competition in armament' (Pigou 1921, p. 23). They sell their products to different countries at the same time. It is enough to induce one government to buy from them to convince another that war is imminent and they should arm themselves. Therefore, as the fear of war may justify the existence of a standing army, it makes war more likely.

Pigou regards the causes that are given to war, such as an insult to the flag or the murder of an official personage, as trivial; he attributes the real reasons for having a strong standing army by a modern nation and the desire to go to war to two main causes; firstly the desire to dominate other nations and the second the desire to acquire economic gains. Though civilised nations 'do not go to war with one another with the vowed and direct purpose of loot ... economic causes also play an important part' (pp. 18, 24). Pigou shares with Ricardo, Say, Engels and Hirst the suspicion of the motivation for going to war. He argues that the main political cause of war is the desire of rulers to dominate others. This desire is for the sake of itself and does not usually represent any strategic interest of the nation. David Ricardo summarised this as the 'stupid jealousy' of rulers at his time. Pigou also agrees with David Ricardo on the long-term impact of war on the structure of the economy. He argues that: 'The essential fact of war-time was that the government got into its own hands, by a combination of taxes, loans and credit creation, the predominant part of the purchasing power of the country. It wielded this purchasing power to direct productive forces towards the common victory. It speeds up the transition from peace organisation to war organisation' (p. 234). He further argues that 'in war public action built national factories where energy was centred on social needs: in peace these factories are sold to profit-seeking private enterprise and at once diverted in large parts to making luxuries' (ibid.). If national resources that had been concentrated in the hands of the government continued during the subsequent peace they could be directed into reconstruction of houses, re-equipping railways and overhauling mines. He argues that the private sector has failed to do these things and squandered national resources for trivial and futile ends. Pigou therefore urges the government to retain some control over the economy for the protection of consumers after the war. Whether or not this control should be extended to the nationalisation of main industries, particularly the railways and mines, or stops short at supervision and regulation was left as an open-ended question during the 1920s but was taken seriously during the Second World War.

It is evident that the political economy tradition that prevailed during the latter part of the 19th century and the first quarter of the 20th century was hostile to high military expenditure on the grounds that although security is paramount for economic prosperity, the consensus was that politicians and rulers were pursuing their own glorification and desire to extend their power over other territories and other nations. The destructive power of war machines experienced during the First World War increased the mistrust of the wisdom of war preparation and the building of strong armies and navies. It was largely agreed that the human and the economic costs of war preparation and actual war itself by far exceeds the resources available for war. A few years after the First World War, Pigou summarised this as follows:

> The sum of real resources available for war, does not, of course, measure the loss that a country which becomes engaged in war may suffer. In any attempt to compute this it would be necessary to take account of the enormous destruction of values outside the economic sphere altogether – the shattering of human promise, the accumulated suffering in wounds and disease of many who go to fight, the accumulated degradation in thought and feeling of many who remain at home – which war almost inevitably involves. Moreover, even if we keep within the economic sphere, it is evident that losses may be inflicted by direct enemy action on parts of the economic body of a country

> that are not, and perhaps could not be, directly mobilised for war. For instance, in a country invaded by an enemy, much private property may be destroyed in the actual operations of war. In a country which is not invaded great losses may be inflicted upon many people through the interference with foreign trade which war involves (p. 45).

Unfortunately, the peace following the First World War didn't last long and the problem of rebuilding Europe was exacerbated by economic decline and eventually by the Great Depression of the 1930s. The peace treaties signed between the major warring European countries at the end of the First World War were not satisfactory to everyone, especially not to Germany. The tension between European countries started to grow gradually and Germany was not short of political and economic grievances, leading it to start a new and more devastating war in 1939. Unlike other previous wars, the new war led to two distinctive technological and human outcomes; firstly, the advent and use of the nuclear bomb and secondly the devastating human costs which culminated in ethnic cleansing and the extermination of the European Jews. Though the second consequence of the war was by no means related to military expenditure or the advances in military technology, it certainly made war an uncivilised and abhorrent human activity.

In the aftermath of the Second World War, the world became dominated by two hostile superpowers, the US and the USSR. In addition to the fierce arms race between the two, the superpowers divided the rest of the world into friendly and hostile countries. The end of the war also coincided with the independence of many developing countries. These countries relied heavily on developed countries for economic aid and trade. Given the international political atmosphere, it was easy for these politically weak and economically poor countries to align themselves with superpowers. Indeed, the superpowers deliberately targeted developing countries for alliance through aid, trade and *coups d'état*.

The arms race between the two superpowers further advanced the extent and the scale of armaments. The revolution in military technology, with such advances in nuclear bombs, ballistic missiles and nuclear-powered submarines, made the next expected war the most feared and the ultimate doomsday catastrophe. The possibility of a devastating war which may involve the use of a nuclear bomb occupied the mind of peace campaigners, humanists, womens' organisations and ordinary people alike. Economists, however, became alarmed by the huge increase in military expenditure and its opportunity costs to the welfare and development of developing countries.

Military expenditure and the economies of the developing countries

Many developing countries, particularly African countries, gained their independence after the Second World War. Most, if not all, started with limited financial resources, poor infrastructure and limited access to external financial resources. Furthermore, in a competitive international commodity market, the developing countries had limited power to influence the price of their exports. It was not until the first oil-price rise in the early 1970s, when some developing countries gained the upper hand in the commodity market, that this influence increased, which inspired other non-oil commodity producers. However, the post-independence era in developing countries' politics was marred by the dominance of the military. Until early 1980s, military *coups d'état* dominated the political life in most developing countries. There is no doubt that the rise of the political influence of armed force in the developing countries during the 1970s and 1980s coincided with the rise of military expenditure in those countries. In general, the developing countries, through various means, increased their share of world military expenditure during the 1950s and early 1970s. Table 2.3 shows that the share of developing countries in world military expenditure increased from as little as 6.2 per cent in 1955 to about 21.3 per cent in 1975. The Middle Eastern countries experienced the largest average increase.

The rise of military expenditure during this era can be attributed to a variety of factors. Some are institutional, and others are due to changes

Table 2.3 World military expenditure: growth rates and percentage distribution, 1955–75

	Annual change (%)	1955	1960	1965	1970	1975
NATO	1.0	61.7	62.3	55.2	49.9	44.8
USA	0.5	46.2	45.5	39.3	37.2	30.0
WTO	3.3	29.4	27.3	30.5	33.7	33.3
USSR	2.8	27.4	25.0	27.7	30.1	28.5
Other Europe	3.4	1.6	1.8	1.8	1.4	1.5
Other developed	4.1	1.2	1.1	1.3	1.4	1.5
China	6.5	2.9	3.1	4.9	5.7	6.1
All developing	10.3	6.2	10.2	14.9	17.9	21.3
Middle East	16.7	0.5	0.8	1.1	2.2	6.1
World total	2.6	100.0	100.0	100.0	100.0	100.0

Sources: SIPRI, *Yearbook* (1976); Ball (1988).

in the economic fortunes of some developing countries. A large portion of this increase can be attributed to the dramatic increase in Middle Eastern military expenditure triggered by the quadrupling of oil prices during early 1970s. Table 2.4 shows that initially the Middle Eastern countries had very little military expenditure. Though the risk of full military confrontation between Israel and its neighbouring countries remained very high during late 1960s and 1970s, the rise of the region's military expenditure was largely due to the unprecedented rise in oil prices rather than any other factors. The oil-exporting countries of the region suddenly ended up with enormous proceeds from their oil exports. The low absorption capacity of the economies of the oil-exporting countries meant that a large proportion of that revenue was spent on building huge government apparatus, including large military and security forces. The most intriguing observation here is that the nominal rise in crude oil prices during 1970s was about 400 per cent while the rise in military expenditure was about 1400 per cent.

Notwithstanding this, military expenditure generally increased across the developing countries during the 1960s and 1970s. As Ball (1988) argues, approximately two-thirds of the developing countries gained their independence after the 1950s. Since many of those countries didn't have a domestic military force of their own before independence, they naturally established defence and security forces as part of their nation-building effort. Unlike other governmental institutions or other sectors of the economy, the armies of the developing countries relied heavily on external sources of weaponry. Therefore, their expenditure started to absorb a substantial proportion of their national income and subsequently a large portion of their export earnings. Another reason for the increase in military expenditure during 1970s was the increase in the exports of developing countries. The herding effect of the rise in oil prices led to a rise in the price of other primary commodities – the main exports of the developing countries. Another reason for the high military expenditure of developing countries was their increased access to hard currencies required for importing weaponry at a time of a decline in military as well as developmental assistance from developed countries. The US, through the Marshall Plan, extended substantial amounts of aid to Western Europe after the Second World War. As the European Recovery Programme achieved its main objectives, there was a strong incentive to direct aid to the developing countries. US and the European aid was originally oriented towards propping up shaky regimes around the world against the rise of the influence of the USSR. It is equally true that Eastern European aid was also aimed at supporting friendly political

Table 2.4 Military expenditure in the developing world, constant prices ($1,000)

Region	1955	1960	1970[1]	1980[2]	1993[3]	2000	2005[4]
Middle East	595	1,035	4,570	63,240	46,832	51,700	63,000
South Asia	935	1,030	2,237	6,803	11,876	19,900	25,000
Far East	1,770	2,800	5,870	31,352	62,626	95,500	120,000
Oceania	687	624	1,332	3,874	7,506	9,500	11,500
Africa	150	305	1,918	17,511	11,310	11,100	12,900
C. America	210	340	618	3,705	1,712	3,600	3,200
S. America	1,200	1,320	2,110	10,950	9,210	17,800	20,600
Total	5,547	7,454	18,655	137,435	151,072	209,100	256,200

Notes: 1. 1955, 1960 and 1970 data is at 1970 prices exchange rates.
2. At 1986 prices and exchange rates.
3. At 1990 prices and exchange rates.
4. 2000 and 2005 data is at 2003 prices and exchange rates.

Sources: SIPRI, *Yearbook* (1976, 1988, 1996, 2002, 2006).

regimes amongst developing countries. For both camps aid was used as a means of political leverage rather than for promoting economic development. Although the OECD official development assistance (ODA) aimed at a target of 0.7 per cent of GNP, it never reached that level. Indeed, the level of aid started to decline from 0.51 percent in 1960 to 0.36 percent in 1975 (Williamson and Milner 1991). Ball (1988) argues that military grants were particularly important during the 1960s and 1970s in enabling the newly independent developing countries to build armed forces that could not have been supported if these countries were relying solely on their domestic resources. Military aid during that period also created a lucrative market for the armament industries of the developed countries and as aid and grants were reduced during 1970s and 1980s, the newly created markets for armaments started to pay off.

This alarming increase of the allocation of vast amounts of world resources to the military and to armaments became a serious cause for concern amongst economists and other scholars. In economic literature, it led to the development of a very important strand of argument related to the economic benefits of disarmament – the so-called *peace dividend*. It was argued that high military expenditure would have an adverse effect on economic growth and welfare. The argument is largely based on the premise that high military expenditure would crowd out other types of public expenditure such as health services, education, poverty reduction and other types of social services. Though the exposition of models of the peace dividend paradigm is not our purpose at this stage, the end of the cold war and the sudden collapse of the USSR and the WTO made the magnitude of the peace dividend a significant issue. The concept of the peace dividend itself refers to the benefits a country gains from lowering its military expenditure. Since the military diverts resources from the productive sectors of the economy to non-productive activities – as argued by classical economists – it is logical to assume that the ultimate and long-term benefits of downsizing the military will eventually outweigh the short-term costs that the process of readjustment entails. A typical peace dividend that economists have thought of is the release of human and capital resources that could be reinvested in the production of goods and services that are destined for civilian use. The perceived magnitude of the peace dividend has been the subject of many studies in the past 10 to 15 years. Amongst them, the peace dividend studies by Gleditch et al. (1994), Gleditch et al. (1996), Clements et al. (1998) and Davoodi et al. (1999) stand out.

It is beyond the scope of this chapter to go through the main strands of literature about the significant economic and social benefits or otherwise of the peace dividend; for the developed countries, however, the weight of the economic argument amongst economists was in favour of disarmament. The theoretical underpinning of this argument, at least from an economic theory point of view, is still the misallocation of resources to unproductive activities. The political argument for the peace dividend, however, is supported by the expected benefits of economic and political collaboration rather than military confrontation. Undeniably, the threat to humanity of a nuclear confrontation between East and West was far from a remote possibility in the political environment that prevailed in the aftermath of the Second World War. However, the extension of the general framework to the developing countries is less clear-cut.

The distinction between the developed and developing countries in this regard rests on the availability of resources and the nature of military expenditure itself. The developing countries are largely perceived to be resource-scarce countries particularly during the period when most of the developing countries gained their independence from the colonial powers. Since the military diverts resources from productive to non-productive economic activities, the conclusion was that the more resources are allocated to the military and defence, the less they will be available for building the civilian economy and therefore high military expenditure will have a negative effect on economic growth and welfare. The other distinction between military expenditure in developed and developing countries is the lack of well-developed defence industries in the developing countries, particularly during the early independence period. This means that they have to rely on foreign sources for their armaments. At this early phase of economic development, large import bills induced by high military expenditure result in balance of payment deficits and inevitably a reduction in the imports of other essential growth-inducing capital goods. The overall effect of high military expenditure therefore has a negative effect on economic growth and welfare.

Many of the empirical studies of the relationship between military expenditure and economic growth flourished during 1970s as the result of, and in response to, Benoit's seminal and controversial works (1973, 1978). Benoit examined the effects of military expenditure, taking into account investment rates, foreign aid receipts and certain other variables in 44 countries between 1950 and 1965. Contrary to expectations, he found out that countries with a heavy defence burden generally had the most rapid rate of economic growth and those with a lower defence burden tended to have lower growth rates. Benoit concluded that the direction of causality runs from defence expenditure to growth rather than vice versa. He argued that defence expenditure makes a tangible contribution to civilian economies by: 1) feeding, clothing, and housing a number of people who would otherwise have to be fed, housed, and clothed by the civilian economy; 2) providing education and medical care as well as vocational and technical training; 3) engaging in a variety of public works – roads, dams, river improvements, airports, communication networks; and 4) engaging in scientific and technical specialities.

Benoit's findings have been the subject of intense theoretical and empirical criticism. Though Benoit was not regarded as pro-militarist, his conclusions were certainly supportive of such a position. Smith and Smith (1980) argue that Benoit's regression analysis was not based on an explicit theoretical model. The absence of a clear underlying theoretical framework leads to the rise of the problems of specifications, interpretation and treatment of simultaneity. For instance, the choice and the interpretation of variables included in his regression analysis were not appropriate. They argue that Benoit calculated the growth in civilian output as the real rise in GDP minus the real growth in military expenditure; the correct formula should have included the ratio of the level of GDP to the level of civilian output. In addition, Benoit did not consider the different rates of population growth or the different levels of economic development of the countries covered by his regression, which ranged from Greece and Spain to Burma and Ceylon. Furthermore, they argue that rates of growth of GDP and civilian output are inadequate indicators of the rate of development. On the same point Ball (1983) argues that Benoit's study was carried out in a socio-political vacuum. East-West politics and competition and their influence on the developing countries' military expenditure were not considered. Ball also argues that Benoit's conclusions did not depend particularly on the results of his regression analysis but on his assessment of non-quantifiable contributions made by military expenditure to the civilian economy. Furthermore, she argues that the effects of those non-quantifiable growth inputs are highly debatable.

Conceptual criticism also includes the test of causality of the direction of effects of military expenditure to economic growth. Joerding (1986) applies the Granger test to data on military spending and growth for 57 developing countries between 1962 and 1977 and finds that the hypothesis of Granger non-causality from growth to military expenditure to be rejected while the hypothesis of Granger non-causality from military expenditure to economic growth is not rejected by data. His conclusion is that empirical studies of the relationship between military expenditure and economic growth have assumed that military expenditure is exogenous with respect to economic growth and, since it is not, they have arrived at incorrect conclusions. In separate studies Chowdhury (1991) and Kusi (1995) use the same methodology to analyse the presence and direction of causality between economic growth and military expenditure using different sample periods. Both studies arrive at the conclusion that the relationship between military expenditure and economic growth cannot be generalised across countries. The actual relationship may vary from one country to another due to factors such as the use of different sample periods, differences in socio-economic structure and types of government in each country. The last two studies reject the uniform application of the same analytical methodology used by Benoit across countries. This principle of uniform application of models across countries has also been rejected by studies by Biswas (1993), Biswas and Ram (1986), Landau (1994), Frederiksen and Looney (1982) and Looney (1993). These studies have found that the significant relationship between military expenditure and economic growth depends on whether the countries are resource-scarce or resource-abundant.

Perhaps the most serious problem with Benoit's study is its implicit political implications for developing countries. Its conclusion of a positive correlation between military expenditure and economic growth implicitly supports the role of the military in politics and economic decision-making in developing countries, while the consensus amongst researchers is that conclusion drawn from such a simple and controversial econometric model is inadequate in explaining the complex relationship between economic growth and military expenditure. Indeed, the social and political impacts of military expenditure are so complex, it would be highly simplistic to have it captured in a single econometric model.

Despite the aforementioned difficulties with Benoit's theoretical and technical framework, researchers have not ruled out a spin-off effect from military expenditure on economic growth. Since then, literature on the subject has flourished tremendously. Dunne (1996) and Smith (2000) provide an extensive list of models that suggest various possible channels through which military expenditure may influence output. For our purpose, it suffices here to briefly list the possible effects of military expenditure.

1) Direct effects: This includes the demand effects suggested by Benoit. It is argued that higher military expenditure will increase the demand for goods and services and stimulates the economy through the Keynesian multiplier effect. The assumption is that underutilisation of resources and military expenditure increases utilisation and reduces the underemployment of resources in the economy. In the majority of developing countries, underutilisation, particularly in the labour market, does exist; however, other resources, particularly finance, are generally scarce. Ultimately, governments that face a budget constraint have to either raise finance for military expenditure through internal sources or seek external sources of finance. Internal sources of finance include raising taxes, increasing money supply or reducing other types of government expenditure. The scope for raising taxes is limited in developing countries and it is socially undesirable. Therefore, the governments of developing countries may opt for increasing money supply. The last internal policy option of reducing other types of government expenditure largely comes at the expense of social services. External sources of military financing include borrowing and military aid. The possible implication of raising finance for military expenditure is an increase in inflation and interest rates. Given the supply constraints of many developing economies, this would inevitably have a crowding effect on private investment.
2) Resource mobilisation effects: It is argued that military expenditure may increase resource mobilisation particularly during periods of perceived external threat. The military trains conscripts in a variety of professions other that military training itself. These include, as Benoit argues, the operation and repair of vehicles, aircraft and radios;

training in hygiene and medical care and in construction methods that may have high civilian utility. It is also argued that military R & D may have commercial spin-offs.

3) Open economy effects: Armament imports may reduce the imports of other essential goods such technology, medicine and other growth-inducing commodities. This type of crowding out is more serious in the case of developing countries that face low international demand for their exports.
4) Security provision: It has long been argued that the provision of security by the military is vital for investment and economic growth. Though high military expenditure doesn't necessarily lead to a greater sense of political stability, the security of persons and property has a profound impact on foreign investment decision-making. However, as Dunne et al. (2005) have noted, in many cases military expenditure may be driven by rent-seeking rather than security *per se*. The military class in developing countries is usually powerful enough to extract the highest budget from the government. This class also has a strong connection to the internal and external military industrial complex. Their combined influence on the governments of the developing countries may form a strong driving force behind high military expenditure.

The abovementioned possible effects of military expenditure on the economy show that positive effects of military expenditure may be offset by its negative effects. It is also worth noting that military expenditure in developing countries is largely used as political leverage rather than as an economic instrument. Many econometric models that have examined the relationship between military expenditure and the economy in the past 30 years or so ignore the political and social complexity of the relationship. Unfortunately, the positive spillover effects of high military expenditure on demand has been receiving more attention than the possible negative socio-economic effects. Factors that have generally been ignored include:

1) East-West rivalry has had a profound effect on international political development since the end of the Second World War. Since then, there is hardly a developing country that has not been touched by the conflict between superpowers. Military aid to developing countries has been a powerful and to a large extent an effective political instrument widely used by the superpowers. Many African and Middle Eastern countries are still victims of that policy and there is no doubt that

the humanitarian tragedy of the horn of Africa in the past quarter of a century has been mainly caused and fuelled by that rivalry rather than anything else.

2) The role of the military class in income distribution has largely been ignored. In most developing countries, the military has been very reluctant to relinquish its grip on power in favour of civilian administration. The recent history of the last half of the 20th century is riddled with examples of brutal military dictatorships; most were condoned if not directly supported by developed countries.
3) The role of the military industrial complex in the armaments trade and the promotion of high military expenditure. The military industrial complex has developed a considerable relationship with governments in developed countries. It uses various lobbying channels to influence public policy regarding the production, the sale and the advancement of certain foreign policies that may not be conducive to the development of the economies of the developing countries. Since the sale of armaments is regulated by governments through export licences, governments of developed countries also champion the cause of military industry with foreign governments. Although the main causes of militarisation may be traced to internal and regional economic and political conflicts, armaments imports have undoubtedly exacerbated potential conflicts. It is enough to convince a government in a volatile region to buy a consignment of bombs and missiles to open the market for further sales and trigger an arms race between opposing countries. It is not uncommon to find two rival countries buying the same type of weaponry from a single source. Allegations of bribery in the Al-Yamama arms deal between the UK government and Saudi Arabia is testimony of the influence of the arms industry on government decision-making. The 'unwarranted influence' of the military industrial complex, to use President Eisenhower's expression, could extend beyond the simple armament procurements by dictatorial and undemocratic regimes in developing countries. The compound economic and social implications of this influence are underestimated in the literature.

Military expenditure and the economies of the Middle East

As one of the most highly militarised regions of the world, the Middle East has attracted the attention of military strategists as well as economic practitioners. Broadly speaking, there have been three distinctive statistical approaches to the study of the relationship between high military expenditure and economic growth in the region. Firstly, the Granger causality test of the direction of the relationship between military expenditure and economic growth. Looney and Winterford (1995), Al-Yousif (2002), and Abu-Qarn and Abu-Bader (2003) fall into this category. Secondly, statistical models built on the works of Biswas and Ram (1986) Yildirim et al. (2005) and Cohen and Ward (1996) employ such a model which is designed largely to capture a positive relationship between the two. The third approach uses the Harrod-Domar neoclassical growth model. Askari and Corbo (1974) and Gottheil (1974) have employed some variants of this model.

Perhaps the main major empirical study of the economic causes and consequences of defence expenditure in the Middle East is a book by Looney and Winterford (1995). The authors employ the Granger methodology to test the causality direction between military expenditure and economic growth. The countries covered by the study are Algeria, Egypt, Syria, Israel, Saudi Arabia and Pakistan over various sub-periods between 1955 and 1988. The authors find that, aside from Pakistan, there is little evidence that defence hurts investment and growth. However, when the authors examine the relationship between military expenditures and human capital development, they find, albeit with reservations, that military expenditure appears to retard human capital development in the region. However, Al-Yousif (2002) looks at defence spending and economic growth in six Arab Gulf countries using a similar method and has found that neither growth nor defence can be considered exogenous and the relationship between the two cannot be generalised across countries. Abu-Qarn and Abu-Bader (2003) also examine government expenditure, military spending and economic growth in Egypt, Israel and Syria using causality evidence and find that the military burden has negatively affected economic growth for all three countries in the past three decades.

Within the second empirical framework, Yildirim et al. (2005) investigate the relationship between military expenditure and economic growth in the Middle East. They use cross-section and dynamic panel estimation techniques covering different income group countries in the region. They reach a conclusion that military expenditure enhances economic growth in the region. Cohen and Ward (1996) use a similar model covering the 1951–93 period and suggest that military spending is beneficial for economic growth throughout a cross-section of the Middle East. The authors, however, acknowledge that despite the strong link found, military spending entails huge opportunity costs that may be easy to ignore in a simple analysis but should not be underestimated.

Askari and Corbo (1974), look at the economic implications of military expenditure in the Middle East during the 1960–9 period. This is an early assessment of the potential contribution of resources to non-military output which have been utilised for military purposes. The study uses the Harrod-Domar growth model. It calculates the accumulated loses in terms of GNP of individual countries (in millions of US dollars at 1960 prices) and reaches a conclusion that the sum of losses as a percentage of combined GNP of the region was equal to 47 per cent during the period covered. Gottheil (1974) also employs a similar model and concludes that there is substantial economic growth gain from the normalisation of military expenditure to its level in Latin American countries.

The conclusion from the overall empirical studies on the relationship between military expenditure and economic growth is that the findings of studies are dependent on the theoretical and empirical framework followed. Though none of the approaches seriously consider the opportunity costs of military expenditure and the destructive consequences of military conflict on the economy of the region, the models which are based on the Harrod-Domar growth framework are more likely to emphasise the existence of the trade-off between military and non-military output and growth.

Conclusion

The question of having a standing army poses a huge burden on a society's resources. At best, when peace prevails, the standing army would remain idle without having any economic output at all. At worst, conflicts that involve the army, whether in low-level border skirmishes or a full-blown war, will strengthen militarisation and encourage more spending on defence. Defence in many regions of the world is self-perpetuating and an increase in the defence expenditure of one country is likely to set off high defence spending in neighbouring countries if not leading to a full arms race. A strong army itself can act like a 'black hole' that acts independently to suck in resources from other sectors of the economy. In many countries, the military budget is so sensitive that it is the last part of the government budget to be reduced by policy-makers in the face of an economic downturn. Even without being engaged in conflicts, the state seems to require a standing army to provide the psychological environment for peace and stability. Switzerland is a very good example in this respect. The country has not been engaged in any conflict in the past half a millennium but maintains one of the most expensive standing armies of the world.

As discussed earlier, the primordial call for protection from potential enemies has been emphasised in literature since Adam Smith. Defence, however, has now surpassed its conventional meaning. It no longer means protecting the nation within its internationally recognised borders. Many countries, particularly the economically and politically powerful ones, send their armies far and wide to chase real or imaginary enemies around the world. In the developing countries, it has also acquired a social and political dimension. In many countries the military is an instrument of state power, social influence and cohesion, and an economic magnet for particular classes. Consequently military expenditure has grown dramatically and the economic burdens of defence have gone beyond the simple imperative security costs to nations. According to SIPRI, world military expenditure in 2006 was estimated to be $1204bn at current prices. This represents an increase of 3.5 per cent in real terms since 2005 and a 37 per cent rise over the 10-year period since 1997. This huge economic burden has posed a moral dilemma for academics and many policy-makers alike. While some measure of spending on defence is regarded as vital for the provision of security, finding an acceptable level of spending on defence has become a complex social and political Holy Grail. Since defence spending is governed by many internal and external factors, there is no consensus between researchers as to how much is acceptable and how much is too much to spend on defence.

In addition, the theoretical and empirical literature reviewed in this chapter shows that there is a considerable disagreement between practitioners as to whether military spending promotes or hinders economic growth and development. The issue has become more controversial since Benoit's seminal work during the early 1970s. Modern defence literature also either underestimates or considers as negligible the socio-political effects of military expenditure and military conflict. These effects are rarely discussed in the context of modern empirical studies of the impact of military expenditure. It is also worth mentioning that the availability of reliable data on the full costs (budgetary and opportunity costs) has also posed a dilemma. Defence data, particularly in developing countries, is shrouded with secrecy and riddled with inaccuracy. Under-reporting or over-reporting and double-counting are also quite common. Though this shortcoming of data is widely acknowledged by empiricists, the study of the effects of military expenditure and military conflict are largely considered as a form of applied economics. Therefore it is reasonable to state that the empirical studies that are based on such unreliable data are not expected to lead to sensible analytical conclusions. Another shortcoming of modern defence economics is that it does seldom pay attention to how politics influences economic behaviour or how the state as an embodiment of politics influences resource allocation to defence. Subsequently, modern defence economics is almost completely divorced from the historical and political developments of societies.

The approach that is adopted in following chapters takes into consideration the afore-mentioned controversies. The country case studies do not discuss military expenditure and defence in isolation from political developments in those countries. We believe that spending on military and military conflicts are above all political decisions and have been taken primarily for political reasons. The outcomes of those decisions have profound implications for the economic and social wellbeing of all social classes in a society. Therefore, the following chapters will first investigate the emergence and the historical role of the armies as instruments of political and social power and then discuss and analyse the available data on military expenditure.

The theoretical perspective of this study is that conflict resolution through political means and the reduction of hostilities between nations are expected to lead to a reduction in military expenditure in the long term. The release of resources from that reduction is generally expected to lead to the so-called peace dividend. However, there is a broad consensus among economists that this can only be realised if the reduction of militarism and military expenditure are brought about by governments which aim to utilise the resources released from defence for developmental purposes. We would, however, not assume that the resources that are released from military expenditure reduction would automatically be translated into higher economic growth and improvements in the welfare of ordinary people. In some cases, the gains may also not be distributed equally between social classes. There is no doubt, however, that socially responsible governments would extract more benefits out of the released resources.

3
Iran: The Quest to Become the Dominant Regional Power

The military and the state

Unlike many developing countries, Iran was never colonised by a colonial power nor was its army established by a European colonial power. At the turn of the last century, Iran was ruled by the weak dynasty of the Qajars and the central government's rule was hardly extended beyond the capital Tehran. Many provinces, such as Khuzestan, Gilan, and Khorasan, largely governed their own affairs. The core of the modern army in the country was originally established by Russian Cossack officers in 1879. In 1920, two other semi-military forces existed along side the small Cossack armed force. The first was the gendarmerie which was created by Swedish officers in 1911 and second was the Persia Rifles of about 6,000 men created by Great Britain in the south of Iran. By the end of the First World War, the Cossack army was just about 8,000 men. The Russian Revolution of 1917 weakened the Russian influence in Iran and the British assumed more power and started supporting the Cossack's small army. In February 1921, the British government encouraged Colonel Reza Khan to march on Tehran and in a bloodless coup he seized power. Reza Khan, himself a son of an army officer of no distinguished aristocratic background, eventually deposed Ahmad Mirza, the last Qajar Shah, in 1925 and crowned himself as the new Iranian Shah and changed his name to Reza Shah Pahlavi as the founder of a new dynasty.

Reza Shah's success in unifying the country under a centralised government relied heavily on the army and the gradual increase in the country's oil revenues. The new Shah quickly realised the potential of his army for keeping the country unified through its use as a tool to subdue dissent. He clearly needed a strong army to impose the central government's policies on the unintegrated regions and for resisting interventions from foreign powers. Reza Shah was fully aware of the weakness of the previous ruling dynasty. The previous dynasty (1796–1925) was too weak to refuse the neighbouring countries various military, trade and economic concessions. To avoid this fate, Reza Shah started building his army even before assuming complete power in 1925. In 1922 the army rose from a few thousand soldiers under his command to 40,000 and its budget was increased to about half of the government's spending. By 1941, the year he was removed from power, the unified army stood at 125,000 (Halliday 1979). To build a modern army, Reza Shah built two military schools in Tehran, established a small air force in 1924 and a navy in 1932. Despite all these, the Shah's leaning towards Nazi Germany put him in a very precarious position with the West. As Russia declared war against Germany in 1941, the Allied powers wanted to use Iran as a bridge for sending military and food aid to Russia and the Shah allegedly refused to allow this; therefore, Allied forces invaded the country and the Shah was forced into exile. In his place, his son Mohamed Reza was made Shah.

The 1940s was a crucial decade in the history of the Iranian army; on the one hand a powerful relationship was established between the army and the US, and on the other hand the army established itself as a formidable force for internal suppression. As the Allied force invaded the country the US brought in 30,000 army personnel, largely to work on transporting supplies to Russia. The US used the opportunity of its presence in Iran to rebuild the army and establish a long-lasting relationship with the most important instrument of power in Iran. In 1941 and 1942, it brought two small missions which were assigned advisory and operational roles in the army. This relationship became paramount for the US as anti-communist activity took a central significance in the US's foreign policy after the war. Weary of the influence of the Russians and the British ambitions in the country, the Iranian government also wanted to use the US relationship to counterbalance the weight of the last two. The US gradually consolidated it presence in the country by extending military and advisory assistance to the army. The relationship between Iran and the US was cemented further as the confrontation between the nationalists lead by Prime Minister Mossadeq and international oil companies led to the military coup on 19 August 1953. The army took a central role, albeit with US support, to reinstate the Shah in power in the coup and removed Prime Minster Mossadeq from office.

By the beginning of the 1970, the army had developed into a formidable controlling state institution. In the absence of a modern structure of a state in the form of public representation and some basic forms of democracy, the army's role was socially and politically reinforced by the desperate need of the Shah for a loyal instrument of power. Unlike its neighbouring Arab armies, which controlled political, social and economic life for far too long under the pretext of liberating Palestine, the Iranian army had little reason to retain its strong grip on power beyond supporting the Shah's economic and political strategies.

The Shah's regime lacked political legitimacy, particularly after the second military coup in 1953. The central theme that the regime promoted was the revival of Iran's ancient imperial image as a regional power that could rival other nations in the region. This central theme of government suited the US's interest in preventing the Russians from extending their influence southwards and was also essential for guaranteeing the security of the weak sheikhdom city-states in the Gulf region. Therefore, the strong relationship between the Shah's government and the US was based on mutual interests. On the one hand, the internally weak government of the Shah required a strong foreign economic and military patron. On other hand, the US's alarm about the possibility of a Russian expansion in the region as well as security in the Gulf region made its influence on the Shah's government a viable alternative to its direct presence. In this equation, arming Iran had a profound importance for the US. In its relationship with Iran, the US government ignored the repressive, paranoid and undemocratic nature of the Shah's regime and extended its most sophisticated armaments and logistics to the Iranian army. By the end of the 1970s, the US had tens of thousand of advisors in the country and it was envisaged that the number would increase to 60,000 personnel by the beginning of the 1980s. The US also agreed to sell modern conventional armaments, including F-14 and F-15 combat fighter jets, to the country.

The massive sale of armaments was fuelled by the quadrupling in the price of oil in the early 1970s and a consequent massive increase in the state's oil revenue. One of the paradoxes of the Shah's regime was that despite its close relationship with the US and Europe, it pursued a hawkish policy in the oil market. However, unlike the Kingdom of Saudi Arabia, Iran, with a population of 36 million during the mid-1970s, had a relatively large absorption capacity for windfall oil revenue, a large share of which was spent on buying unnecessary and militarily unjustified modern and sophisticated armaments from the US. The acquisition of highly advanced weaponry systems created an illusory sense of power and security for the regime to the extent that it neglected all but essential non-military public expenditure. Wary of public discontent, the Shah, backed by massive oil revenue and US military support, envisaged that

Iran would become the fifth most powerful state in the world by the mid-1980s.

Another and perhaps a lesser cause of high military expenditure in the country was the rivalry with its western neighbour Iraq for hegemony over the Gulf region, navigation rights on the Shatt al Arab waterway and the demarcation of the Persian Gulf's continental shelf, crucial for future oil discovery. Though the Iraqi government made conciliatory gestures towards resolving the disputes diplomatically during the civilian Prime Minster Bazzaz's visit to Tehran in 1967, the tone of the diplomatic gesture was strongly opposed by the Iraqi army. Instrumental in this border dispute between the two countries was Iranian support for the Kurdish rebellion in the north of Iraq. In 1968, the pan-Arab Ba'ath party came to power in Iraq eager to foster, at least rhetorically, the Arab causes of conflict with the West and against their arch-enemy Israel. Iraq quickly forged strategic defence and economic relationships with the Soviet Union in early 1970s. In 1972, Iraq signed a 15-year Treaty of Friendship and Cooperation with the Soviet Union. Both Iran and the US became alarmed by the possibility of having a pro-Soviet Union regime in Iraq which could undermine the status quo stability in the Gulf region. The renewed fighting between the Iraqi government and the Kurdish movement in 1974 after four years of uneasy truce gave an opportunity to the Iranian government as well as to the US to exert pressure on the Iraqi regime to come back to the negotiating table. The direct Iranian intervention in assisting the Kurds and the US's open and visible support for them laid the ground for a change in the political and diplomatic climate between the two countries. Iraq categorically refused to make concessions on Kurdish rights as these were regarded as a threat to Iraq's territorial integrity and it was felt concessions would weaken its regional position; it also became deeply entrenched in a prolonged and exhausting war of attrition with the Kurds. After one year of war, Iraq, though reluctant, agreed to make concessions and signed the Algeria Accord with Iran in March 1975. The Accord enshrined Iranian rights and control over the Shatt al Arab and made territorial concessions to Iran based on the 1913 Protocol of Constantinople between the Ottoman Empire and Great Britain, which represented Iran at that time. In return, Iran promised to stop aiding the Kurdish rebellion and to restore security along the common boundaries between the two countries. This Accord boosted the Shah's confidence and his government's reputation as an undisputed regional power.

Though the sense of normality between the two governments was initially at the expense of the Kurds, it also proved to be illusory. Since

Iraq's agreement to the terms and conditions of the Algeria Accord was reluctant, it sought the earliest opportunity to reverse them. The Islamic Revolution in Iran in 1979, which resulted in weakening the army and caused widespread disarray within the official government apparatus, seemed to provide a golden opportunity to the Iraqi government to renege on the Algerian Accord's terms and conditions. Under various pretexts, Iraq invaded Iran in September 1980. In the hope that the demoralised Iranian army would offer little defence and the new rather weak government in Tehran would capitulate quickly, Iraq felt it would be able to redraw the Algerian Accord according to its wishes and impose its terms and conditions on the Iranian government. A quick end to the war also proved to be illusory; the war lasted eight years, with enormous human, social and economic costs for both sides. In 1988 Iran reluctantly agreed on a ceasefire without any formal agreement between the two countries. The disputed issues about border conflicts were left unresolved. Iraq quickly claimed victory by not losing the war, largely because of massive US and European assistance, while Iran lost it by not winning it. By the end of the war, the call for strengthening the army in both countries was as strong as ever.

The Islamic government in Iran was hostile to the US and the European influence by default rather than design. The hostility was largely due to the US's strong support for the corrupt and totalitarian regime under the Shah rather than an ideological difference. The new international relations that the new regime fostered had enormous implications for the army. The US imposed economic and defence embargos on the country and the Iranian army subsequently lost vital sources of armaments and technical support. As a result, the country was forced to resort to the black market and other sources for arms supply.

The end of the war with Iraq did not remove the causes of hostility between the two countries, or indeed in the region. Just three years after the ceasefire between the two countries, Iraq invaded Kuwait and created yet another round of turmoil that embroiled the region in further conflict for ensuing decades. Though Iraq was swiftly evicted from Kuwait, the invasion gave enough pretexts to the US to station its forces in the Gulf on a semi-permanent basis. The consequences of the invasion of Kuwait for the Iraqi army were also devastating. Its armoury was destroyed, its structure weakened, and its sources of weapons cut off. Therefore, Iraq no longer posed a real threat to Iran's security in the short or medium term. The invasion, however, brought the US, the arch enemy of the Islamic government of Iran, to its doorstep.

Though the Islamic rulers of Iran have, at least for the sake of domestic public consumption, portrayed the US as their number one enemy, the threat of a real US intervention became more real after the eviction of Iraq from Kuwait. The US stationed its forces, including air forces, in Saudi Arabia, Kuwait and Qatar. The US also used Incirlik Air Base in Turkey for the enforcement of the no-fly zone in the south and the north of Iraq from 1991 until the fall of Saddam Hussein's regime in 2003. US naval fleets have also had an active presence in the Gulf to protect oil tankers since the mid-1980s, as well as to enforce the economic embargo on Iraq from 1991. Consequently, the Gulf region became one of the most militarised regions of the world.

The invasion of Iraq by the US and its allies at the beginning of 2003 escalated the tension between Iran and the US. Though Iranian military forces have never been a match for US forces in the Gulf, Iran started to carry out covert interventions in Iraq to show that it was a regional player to be reckoned with. In the past few years, the Iranian support of some of the Shi'ite militias has been effective enough to force the US to acknowledge the Iranian role in Iraq and start negotiations with Iran. The invasion of Iraq, however, consolidated the presence of US military forces to an extent that the establishment of permanent or long-term US army bases in the region is more likely than ever. Therefore, Iran's aspiration to become the supreme regional power after the demise of a strong Iraq was dealt a considerable blow. Nonetheless, this fundamental shift in the balance of power has not dented the Iranian government's official strategy and rhetoric about its military capabilities. The current quest for acquiring nuclear technology is part of that strategy and is largely aimed at compensating for the country's weakness in conventional armaments.

The above brief analysis of the some of the conflicts that Iran has experienced shows that, similarly to many other countries of the region, the call for strengthening the army in the country would still find a sympathetic hearing amongst the public and politicians alike. The political turmoil that the country has gone through has been in part instigated by the intervention of external regional as well international forces, and partly has been the result of successive government policies to assert the power of the country in regional politics and the expression of its assumption of the role of a dominant regional power. It should also be said that the geographical position of the country as an important wedge between Russia and the strategically oil-rich Gulf region also played an unfortunate role in raising its stake in the politics of the cold war era. Furthermore, Iranian strategists in both the Shah's government and the Islamic Republic promoted nationalistic rhetoric casting Iran as an ancient, powerful empire matching its rivals both in military and political terms. Surprisingly, this nationalist approach to regional politics has by now replaced the original expansionist Islamic rhetoric of the Islamic revolution of 1979.

The state of the economy

In the past half a century or so, the Iranian economy has undergone three rather distinctive phases of economic development. Each phase has been shaped by particular internal and external socio-political factors.

The first phase started in the early 1960s and lasted until the outbreak of the civil unrest prior to the Islamic Revolution during 1978–9. This phase was marked by a clear and unprecedented transformation of a traditional economy towards a modern one. Despite the government's internal political problems and the growing influence of the US, this era laid down the infrastructure for a modern economy unsurpassed by other developing countries, with the exception of South Korea. Compared with other developing countries, Iran's real growth rate of nearly 9.6 per cent between 1960 and 1977 was roughly double the average of the countries in the middle-income group, and higher than the average growth of any other group of countries of the world (Amuzegar 1993; Halliday 1979). This high growth rate was accompanied by a significant increase in public consumption, an average rise of per capita income by 8 per cent a year, and domestic investment growth of more than 16 per cent a year. This high economic growth was fuelled by the rise in crude oil production and the country's oil revenues. Crude oil exports rose from approximately 1 million barrels a day in 1963 to 5.4 million barrels a day in 1974. By the end of the 1970s, Iran was the second largest oil producer in the world after Saudi Arabia. The aforementioned high growth rates were accompanied by a gradual rise in inflation rates. During the 1960–7 period the inflation rate was 2.5 per cent but started creeping up as consumption and investment increased. It rose to 3.7 per cent during 1968–73. The oil boom of 1973–4 further raised the rate to 15.5 per cent.

For the Shah's government, the influx of oil revenue proved to be a bad omen; the high rates of inflation eroded gains in the standard of living and the economy faced a bottleneck situation. Inadequate and underdeveloped ports, customs, and transportation and communication were hampering imports. Though the country succeeded in the first stage of its import-substitution policy, it remained dependent on foreign sources for its vital capital goods and a substantial proportion of its intermediate goods. The economic boom was also hampered by shortages of skilled labour, raw materials and insufficient electricity supply. The domestic supply constraints, coupled with high public and private demand, brought the economic boom to a halt by 1977. The downturn of the economy was exacerbated by a drop in real oil prices and a decline in the country's oil revenues. Despite the concerted effort by the government to mitigate the adverse economic conditions by revising its economic policies, public discontent by the end of 1978 was increasing to levels that were beyond the control of the government and many of its economic policies were later overtaken by the revolutionary events. The revolution of 1979 effectively halted the unprecedented era of economic boom and structural transformation and ushered the country into an era of political and economic instability.

The second phase started with the outbreak of civil unrest during 1978–9 which later coincided with the outbreak of the war with neighbouring Iraq and lasted until the end of that war in 1988. During this period the economy was affected, to various degrees, by external factors (the war with Iraq and the economic embargo that the US imposed and enforced on the country) and by the internal political turmoil the country was undergoing. In the first few years after the revolution, the power struggle between different political factions was settled, albeit violently and brutally, in favour of the Islamic fundamentalists led by Imam Khomeini.

It is worth mentioning that the economy was on a sliding slope even before the triumph of the revolution. The world recession of 1976–8 led to a decline in the price of oil and in oil revenues of the country. The economic conditions were aggravated by physical constraints (lack of port capacity, warehouses, roads and railways, and the like) and a skill (managerial and technical) bottleneck experienced after the sudden rise in public expenditure during 1973–5. The sudden rise in private and public consumption pushed the inflation rate above 15 per cent in 1976. In this economic downturn, public services were unable to meet the growing needs of an urbanising society, particularly for infrastructure and social services. General shortages, including that of electricity, led to a slowdown of the industrial output of many vital industries. Moran (1978) argues that the energy crisis experienced during 1976 seriously affected industrial production in more than 1,000 plants, including in the country's aluminium smelting, textile, brickmaking, automobile and tractor industries. As a consequence, GDP growth shrank by 1.30 per cent and 7.48 per cent during 1977 and 1978 respectively.

In addition, the revolution brought about a complete break with the old market-oriented and industrialisation policies of the Shah's regime. The new radical policies of the Islamic regime included nationalisation of the country's main industries and of banking and non-banking financial

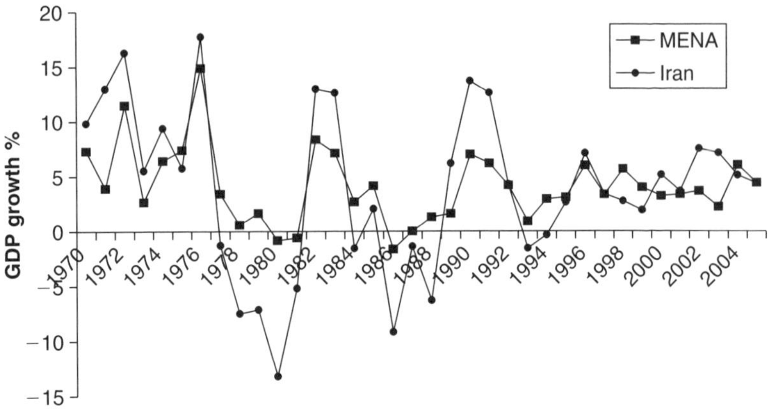

Figure 3.1 GDP growth in Iran and the MENA region, 1970 2005
Source: Calculated from World Bank, *World Development Indicators* (November 2007).

institutions. The new rulers also introduced a firm government grip over prices, consumption, foreign trade and the foreign exchange market. It is worth mentioning that even before the triumph of the revolution in February 1979 the revolutionary turbulence which affected the country for two years led to a massive capital flight, reversing the capital inflow trend stimulated by the expansionary policies of the previous government. The financial shortage was aggravated by the exodus of thousands of entrepreneurs, professionals, business managers and skilled workers.

Unfavourable internal conditions were coupled with the outbreak of the war with Iraq, the economic embargo the US placed on the country after the US embassy hostage crisis and the sharp decline of crude oil prices during the 1980s. This overall turmoil shook the already weak foundations of the economy. Figure 3.1 shows that with the exception of 1982 and 1983, the GDP of the country shrunk during this period. The growth rate of the economy during 1980–9, as Table 3.1 indicates, was –0.3 per cent. Though economic growth across all developing countries, with the exception of the economies of South Asia, was poor during the 1980s, the downturn of the economy in Iran during that decade was exceptionally sharp.

During this period, high rates of inflation coupled with low economic growth led to a marked deterioration in standards of living. Due to the war, economic conditions and the shortage of supplies, the government applied austerity measures to curb consumption, imports and capital flight. Subsequently, per capita GDP as an indicator of living standards

Table 3.1 Average GDP growth in Iran and other regions, selected years, 1970–2005 (%)

	1970–9	1980–9	1990–9	2000–5
Iran	6.12	−0.30	4.60	6.58
MENA	5.97	2.21	4.30	4.50
Latin America	5.71	1.80	2.90	3.70
Sub-Saharan Africa	–	2.18	2.04	4.32
South Asia	3.60	5.70	5.38	7.36
OECD	3.71	2.95	2.48	2.32

Source: Calculated from World Bank, *World Development Indicators* (November 2007).

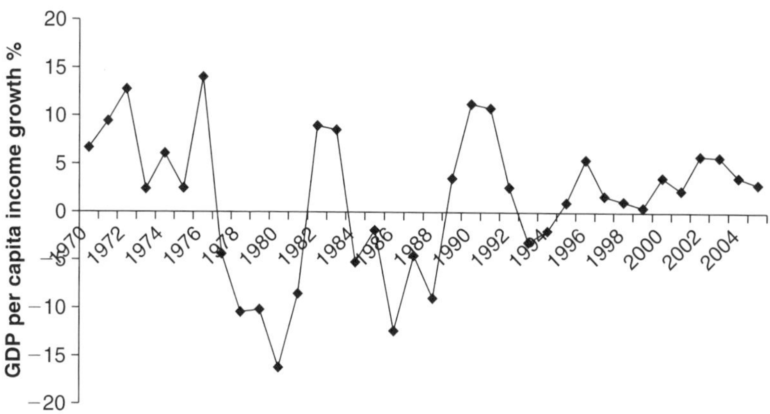

Figure 3.2 Percentage growth of per capita GDP in Iran, 1970–2005
Source: Calculated from World Bank, *World Development Indicators* (2008).

deteriorated sharply during 1978–88. Figure 3.2 shows that with the exception of 1982 and 1983, the growth of per capita income was generally declining. World Bank data show that during that decade, the annual average decline of per capita income amounted to 5.5 per cent. By the end of the period, per capita income was half of its level before the revolution.

The end of the war with Iraq provided an opportunity for economic reform and growth. After the war, the government embarked on a massive economic reform programme aimed at dealing with the aftermath of the war and arresting the downturn in both economic growth and the standard of living of the population. As Hakimian and Karshenas (2000) argue, the aim of the policy reform after the war was to remove some of the market control that the government had undertaken to ease the costs to the public sector, invigorate the private sector and liberalise trade.

By the beginning of the 1990s, crude oil prices picked up and Iran's oil supply increased from 2.369 million barrels a day in 1988 to over 3 million barrels a day in 1990. The rise in crude oil prices improved the total oil revenue of the country. With improved economic conditions, economic growth accelerated to double-digit figures during 1990 and 1991. Though the growth of economy tumbled again during the mid-1990s, largely due to the fluctuation of oil prices, nonetheless the average growth rate during the 1990s matched the growth rate of other Middle East and North African (MENA) countries. The beginning of the new millennium improved the fortunes of the country through high oil prices and a massive oil windfall. In 2006, the oil revenue of the country totalled $59.131bn, which amounts to a ten-fold increase since the mid-1980s. Economic growth therefore increased to an average 6.58 per cent during the period 2004–5.

Military expenditure before the Islamic Revolution of 1979

For almost 35 years, the US carefully nurtured a strong political and military relationship with Iran, starting from the signing of the first military agreement between the two countries on 27 November 1943 until the collapse of the Shah's regime during early 1979. In this period, the US fostered the idea of a strong pro-US and Western European Iranian government. A strong Iranian government was envisaged as providing security for the vital oil supply from the Gulf region. Iran also was situated at the southern flank of the former Soviet Union. The Shah was wary of the Soviet Union's intentions in Iran, particularly after the Soviets' reluctance to withdraw from Iran after the Second World War. This hostility towards the Soviet Union provided a suitable political environment for the US to cement its relationship with the country. As mentioned earlier, a strong pro-US Iran became an indispensable part of a wider US global strategy of containing the spread of communism, particularly to the oil-rich Gulf States. Iran was also regarded by many American strategists as the guarantor of the regional status quo and a counterpoise to emerging radical regimes.

Subsequently, the US became the main provider of armaments hardware and military advice to Iran. It was also important for the US to ensure that the Shah's government did not resort to other sources of armaments, as France and the Soviet Union were eager to compete for Iran's lucrative market, particularly after the dramatic rise in the price of oil during 1973–4.

As argued earlier, the Shah embarked on building a modern army with a capability that went beyond the maintenance of internal security. Though the country's relationship with its western neighbour Iraq improved tremendously after 1975, the Shah's ambition was to build an international status for the country based on a strong and well-equipped army. The Shah's drive was given unconditional support by President Nixon during his visit to Tehran in May 1972. During this visit the National Security Advisor Henry Kissinger agreed for the first time to sell Iran virtually any conventional weapons the Shah wanted. The oil price rise of the 1973 gave the financial impetus to the Shah's military drive. As Table 3.2 shows, military expenditure at the beginning of the 1970s increased dramatically. The rise even started before the major rise in the price of oil. Though that rise coincided with a two-digit economic growth rate in 1971, the rate of the increase was far greater than the growth rate of the economy. According to Klare (1976), between 1970 and 1977, Iran spent $17bn on the purchase of arms from the US and by the mid-1970s, Iran became the largest importer of US military equipment and services. This increase in military expenditure was also matched by an increase in total military manpower. According to Mofid (1990), the total manpower engaged in the army and paramilitary forces increased from 191,000 during 1972–3 to 415,000 during 1979–80. This increase amounts to 117 per cent within six years. In addition, Moran (1978) argues that

Table 3.2 Iran's military expenditure at 1978 prices and exchange rates, 1970–7

Year	Defence budget ($m)	Percentage increase	GDP growth (%)
1970	1,906	–	9.8
1971	1,810	–5.0	13.0
1972	2,518	39.1	16.3
1973	3,467	37.7	5.3
1974	7,664	121.1	9.4
1975	9,731	30.0	5.8
1976	10,557	8.5	17.7
1977	8,573	–18.8	–1.3
1970–7	46,226		

Sources: SIPRI, *Yearbook* (1980, 1981); World Bank, *World Development Indicators* (November 2007).

civilian accounts also included sizable military allocations which were not included in defence spending. For instance, approximately 70 per cent of the public housing outlays were allocated to military construction which amounted to an additional 3 to 5 per cent of the central government's budget.

Table 3.2 indicates that military expenditure increased by more than 3.5 times between 1970 and 1977. On average the country spent $5.778bn per annum during this period. This dramatic rise in expenditure was associated with and fuelled by the sudden rise in the price of oil. Though this rise was curtailed by the end of the Shah's regime, the accumulated costs were already unprecedented. As Moran (1978) argues, the breakneck increase in military expenditure was questionable as a national strategy at the time when the country was not facing an immediate military threat from its neighbours. The pace of modernisation of the army was so fast that it didn't make sense even in narrow military terms. By the mid-1970s, Iran experienced trained pilot and maintenance personnel shortages and the country generally lacked sufficient logistic systems for locating and providing spare parts for highly developed air force units. At some times Iran had more fighter planes than trained pilots. The table also shows a disproportionate rise in military expenditure compared with the growth rate of the economy. The rate of military expenditure for the period 1971–7 was 30.4 per cent whereas the average growth rate in the econmy for the same period was 9.46 per cent.

The above military expenditure figures and other estimates of hidden defence spending which were included in civilian budgets, coupled with about half a million personnel involved in the military, highlights the level of the opportunity cost of the military during the 1970s. Though these figures should be taken as trends rather than final statistics, the indications given show the significance of the army and of militarisation in the Shah's overall strategic plan for Iran. The other inference one would make from the above figures is that the growth of the economy as well as of military expenditure show a strong correlation with the rise of the price of oil in the early 1970s rather than high military expenditure being financed by high economic growth rates. The Shah's drive to buy sophisticated and expensive armaments was largely politically motivated. Iran was not facing an immediate threat of war from any of its neighbours. It is also worth mentioning that the large and sudden increase in military expenditure was well above the management and utilisation capability of the Iranian military forces. This raised concerns among US politicians about the Iranian capability of managing, maintaining and funding current and future armament consignments.

As mentioned earlier, the incapability of Iran to absorb, maintain and manage huge supplies of sophisticated armaments led to the unavoidable presence of thousands of American personnel in Iran, at huge expense and with serious political ramifications.

On the eve of the 1979 revolution, Iranian public opinion was powerfully opposed to the US and the Shah's foreign policy, a vehicle of which was the military and the presence of thousands of American military advisors in the country. Against this background, as Mofid (1990) argues, one of the most important objectives of the Islamic Revolution in 1979 was to reduce Iran's military expenditure and change the country's military orientation and arms imports.

Military expenditure after the Islamic Revolution of 1979

The clergy who seized power in 1979 were hostile to the regular army which was thought to pose a danger to their authority. This hostility stemmed from the US's strong political and military relationship with the Shah's regime. By the end of 1979, the army sustained heavy institutional and personnel blows from the new authorities. Up to 10,000 of its top brass were either executed, imprisoned, dismissed or deserted from the army (Hickman 1982). The command and control structure of the army was also altered by the regime. The new authorities, though not in complete agreement about the role of the army at the beginning of the revolution, generally mistrusted the army. Therefore, clerics were installed in army barracks to monitor and scrutinise the activities of the army and report back to higher Islamic authorities. In this new orientation and the ensuing power struggle between various factions of the revolution, the professional army was denigrated and treated with suspicion. Another important change in the defence strategy, with grave implications for the professional army, was the Islamic doctrine of defence. The new doctrine that the Islamic authorities adopted was based on self-defence, self-reliance and was non-dependent on foreign sources of arms. Contrary to and completely oblivious of modern warfare, the whole defence ethos of the new regime was changed to be based on martyrdom and jihad (holy war). The lack of trust in the professional army led to the creation of a separate paramilitary force which was called the *Pasdaran* – the defenders of Islam formally known as the Iranian Revolutionary Guards Corps (IRGC).

The 1979 revolution ended an important era in the history of the Iranian army which was marked by a clear policy of modernisation and the acquisition of sophisticated Western armaments. The deep-seated hostility of the new rulers towards the professional army also severed the main sources of its weaponry. At the triumph of the revolution, the professional army was reduced to a weak and demoralised institution. Though it kept its newly acquired weaponry, its fighting capabilities were reduced because of the lack of spare parts and professional maintenance, as well as by problems caused by civil upheaval.

Though both Iraq and Iran considered the war between them as defensive, the Iraqi regime used its first successful attacking thrust as a pre-emptive means of forcing the revolutionary rulers in Tehran to come to the negotiating table and halt their call for overthrowing the Ba'ath regime in Baghdad (Karsh 1987). As mentioned earlier, the weakness and the disarray in the Iranian army ranks were exploited by the Iraqi government when they launched their pre-emptive attack. Iraq also sought an opportunity to renege on the terms and conditions of the Algerian Accord of 1975, in which the Iraqi government had made considerable concessions to the Shah's government. The Iran-Iraq war officially started in September 1980 but in reality it was preceded by more than a year of war of words and light skirmishes along the borders between the two countries. In the eight years that the war proper lasted, both countries sustained considerable human, infrastructural and economic losses.

The ramifications of the devastating war for military expenditure and economic growth in Iran were enormous. As Cordesman (1999b) argues, at the triumph of the revolution the ideologues/extremists that came to power were not sure about the amount of resources to be devoted to the professional army. They underestimated the role of modern weaponry in determining the outcome of the war and overemphasised the effectiveness of popular moral force and martyrdom. Iraq's superior equipment and firepower and the West's unequivocal support for it prolonged the war despite the occasional Iranian victory.

The economic costs of the war were colossal by every account. Large areas of western Iran, particularly the oil-rich Khozestan province, were destroyed; this included Iran's most developed petrochemical and oil installations. Iran also lost enormous amounts of oil revenue as the result of the suspension of its oil exports and the destruction of some of its oilfields. The cost of the war to Iran also included the opportunity costs represented by the millions of its workforce who were engaged in the war effort. According to rough estimates, about one million people either lost their lives or were crippled by the war. Iran also incurred other economic costs through resorting to irregular and most of the time very expensive sources of weaponry. Though Mofid (1990) estimates the economic costs of the war to Iran to have been about $452.6bn, the actual costs of the war are almost immeasurable.

By mid-1988, the human, infrastructural and economic costs of the war and the military stalemate made it impossible for either side to win. The Iranian supreme religious leader, Imam Khomeini, became convinced that the war was not winnable and he reluctantly accepted a ceasefire with Iraq. Through the war the army lost its major weapons without significant replacement or re-supply. Despite the economic difficulties the country was experiencing it had to keep its military expenditure relatively high. Table 3.3 shows that even before the revolution the economy shrank by 7.5 per cent, while defence expenditure was kept at 10 per cent of the country's GDP. The revolution ultimately crippled the economy and the economic downturn continued as major restructuring was embarked upon. With the exception of 1982 and 1983, the economy was generally shrinking.

As Table 3.3 shows, the new rulers reduced military expenditure in the first year of the revolution but had to increase it after the war broke out with Iraq. Though these figures must be treated with utmost caution, the table shows that from the beginning of the revolution until the end of the war, Iran spent about $89.340bn, which amounted to an annual average

Table 3.3 Iran's defence expenditure and economic growth at constant 1988 prices and exchange rates, 1978–88

Year	Military expenditure ($m)	Defence spending as % of GDP	GDP growth rate (%)
1978	9,424*	10.0	−7.5
1979	4,757*	−45.5	−7.1
1980	16,108	238.6	−13.2
1981	12,321	−23.5	−5.2
1982	10,230	−17.0	13.0
1983	8,523	−16.7	12.6
1984	8,082	−5.2	−1.6
1985	9,705	20.1	−2.07
1986	9,339	−3.8	−9.2
1987	7,679	−17.8	−1.4
1988	7,353	−4.2	−6.3
1978–88	89,340	–	–

Note: * at constant 1988 price and exchange rates.
Sources: SIPRI, *Yearbook* (1980, 1990); World Bank, *World Development Indicators* (November 2007).

of $8.934bn. It should also be noted that on average the economy shrank by 2.5 per cent annually during this period whereas military expenditure increased by annual average of 12.3 per cent.

Military expenditure after the war with Iraq

After the war, Iran was preoccupied with rebuilding its war-torn economy. The emphasis on offensive military buildup diminished as the threat of an Iraqi military confrontation dissipated, particularly after the First Gulf War. The 1990s, however, brought about other security worries for Iran. The disintegration of the Soviet Union and the independence of Central Asian republics, though not an immediate threat to Iran, became a security worry to the country largely because of the influence of the US and the West on the shaping and defence of those countries. The flaring up of the hostility between Armenia and Azerbaijan is a good example in this context. It is also worth mentioning that the political and military problem in Afghanistan, which escalated into a full-blown invasion by the Allied forces led by the US in 2001, created an uneasy defence environment for Iran. The US also established air bases in Uzbekistan and Kyrgyzstan in 2002 and by 2003 and the US invasion of Iraq, Iran was completely encircled by the US.

With a hostile stance to the US military expansion in the region and the belief that Iranian conventional forces were not a match for the mighty American forces, the Iranian emphasis strategically shifted to focus on the so-called weapons of mass destruction and the development of naval capability to threaten the supply routes of oil in the Gulf region. During the 1990s, Iran was able to import MiG-29 and Su-24 aircraft, T-72 tanks and two Kilo submarines, artillery and surface-to-air missiles from Russia. China and North Korea were also major sources of surface-to-surface missiles for the country. Iran also sought, at least in part, to compensate for the lack of foreign sources of weaponry by building a strong domestic armaments industry.

The data in Table 3.4 indicate that by 1995, military expenditure was about half of its 1985 level. The decrease of military expenditure is also noticeable from the share of defence expenditure of the GNP of the country, which declined from 6.4 per cent in 1989 to 2.6 per cent in 1995. The first Gulf War, however, brought about two strategic changes in the region which Iran became gravely concerned with. Firstly, the war brought the US army into the region. The US stationed some forces in the Gulf countries on a semi-permanent basis. As a consequence, as indicated earlier, Iranian strategists shifted the emphasis to the areas that

Table 3.4 Iran's defence expenditure, economic growth and arms imports, 1989–99

Year	Military expenditure ($m, current)	Defence expenditure as % of GNP	GDP growth rate (%)	Arms imports ($m, current)
1989	7,960	6.4	6.2	1,900
1990	8,260	6.0	13.7	1,900
1991	7,930	5.0	12.6	1,600
1992	5,090	3.0	4.3	850
1993	6,060	3.4	−1.6	1,400
1994	6,030	3.3	−0.4	390
1995	4,930	2.6	2.7	360
1996	5,240	2.5	7.1	370
1997	6,620	3.0	3.4	900
1998	7,050	3.1	2.7	370
1999	6,880	2.9	1.9	150
1989–99	72,050	–	–	–

Sources: WMEAT (2003); World Bank, *World Development Indicators* (November 2007).

posed a serious threat to the Gulf countries and Gulf shipping routes. The data also shows that despite the economic turmoil that the country was experiencing, military expenditure remained at an average of 3.75 per cent between 1989 and 1999, though these figures should be treated as trend rather than absolute figures.

The SIPRI Yearbook (2007) data shows that the military burden, as measured by military expenditure as a percentage of gross domestic product (GDP), excluding the spending on the Revolutionary Guards, started increasing from 2.9 per cent in 1997 to 5.8 per cent in 2005 – a twofold increase in less than ten years. This increase reflects Iranian worries about the tension with the international community over its nuclear programme and the political volatility of the region, particularly after the Allied invasion of Iraq during 2003. The uneasy Iranian relationship with the US and Western European countries has also pushed the country to look east for new sources of weaponry, acquiring long-range missiles from North Korea and offensive aircraft from Russia. Nonetheless, as Table 3.4 indicates, since the end of the war with Iraq, its arms imports have declined considerably. Observers attribute the large value of arms delivery during 1989 to the backlog of arms imports from orders it placed during the war.

Despite the country's difficulties in acquiring modern weaponry, Iran still remains a major conventional military power in the region. It currently has 540,000 men under arms, and more than 350,000 reserves. These include 120,000 members of the IRGC (Cordesman 2006b). In total the country spent $72.05bn in the period 1989–99.

The implications of the nuclear dispute for military expenditure

The Iranian ambition to acquire nuclear technology for peaceful or other purposes goes back to the Shah's era. It started in 1974 when Iran signed an agreement with Germany to build its first nuclear reactor in the Gulf port of Bushehr. Though the reactor was bombed by Iraq during the 1980s war and Germany withdrew from the project, allegedly under US pressure, the Iranian drive to reinvigorate this ambition during the 1990s raised Western as well as regional countries' concerns about Iran's ultimate goal and the consequences of Iran becoming a nuclear power. Though the aim of this section is not to vindicate or vilify Iran for secretly attempting to acquire a nuclear bomb, it is imperative to emphasise that the implications of a nuclear Iran will have far-reaching consequences for the security, stability and militarisation of the region.

The existence of a large-scale nuclear programme for a state well-endowed with oil and gas, together with Iran's failure to disclose certain clandestine nuclear activities to the International Atomic Energy Agency (IAEA) until they were exposed, raise genuine concerns. The Western suspicion is reinforced by the Iranian government's effort to acquire missiles that are capable of delivering nuclear and other warheads, particularly to beyond the borders of its immediate neighbours. The obscurity of the technical issues and disputes about Iran's clandestine nuclear efforts has been exacerbated by the Iranian regime's stance on the US and its allies' presence in the region. This stance was particularly strengthened after the election of Mahmoud Ahmadinejad, a hard-line Islamic fundamentalist, to office in 2005. Iran currently does not recognise the state of Israel and has openly called for its destruction. Jewish lobbies around the world regard President Ahmadinejad's statement in 2005 that Israel should be wiped off the world map as synonymous with a call for the dropping of nuclear bombs on it. Therefore, even if Iran is currently technically unable to produce a nuclear bomb, anti-nuclear Iraq has enough ammunition to sanction Iran economically and seek its complete isolation.

It is obvious that the security advantages of developing independent nuclear technology for Iran are highly contentious; the potential political chaos that it could create is far greater than its alleged benefits. For internal politics the nuclear dispute with the West may have some added benefits for the Ahmadinejad regime as the government has failed to develop the economy and improve standards of living. As Chubin (2006) argues, the ultranationalists/Islamists who are currently in power welcome the return to the state of siege and atmosphere of embattlement experienced in the heyday of the Islamic revolution in 1979. The nuclear dispute with the West and the threat of an immediate confrontation with the US provides an excellent political instrument for suppressing political dissent. Regionally speaking, a nuclear Iran may motivate neighbouring countries such Turkey and Saudi Arabia to acquire a nuclear bomb, with the potential of escalating the Greco-Turkish arms race. The clear conclusion is that the unforeseen consequences of the nuclear dispute for the militarisation of the region are far greater than what had been expected; it is a needless problem that could have been avoided. It has also added an extra source of political and economic instability which will weaken the region's position in the world.

Conclusion

This chapter analysed the origin of the professional army and military expenditure in Iran. Despite the scarcity and the unreliability of data on the issue, currently available data from different sources indicate that the country has spent enormous amounts of resources on military expenditure. It is also important to mention that though the war with Iraq was externally imposed on the country, the Islamic clergy who took power in 1979 were also partly responsible for the outbreak of the war. The war led to huge economic and human capital losses to both countries, but it equally provided an opportunity for the Islamic regime to consolidate its power internally and eliminate opposition.

Karshenas and Hakimian (2005) show that, relative to other countries of the region and even to South Korea, Iran had a magnificent chance to develop and industrialise in the mid-1970s. Unfortunately, that chance was hijacked and disastrously aborted by the irrational misadventures of both the Shah and the reactionary theocratic government that replaced him. As a result of militarisation, regime change and the war with Iraq, the standard of living represented by per capita income at the beginning of the new millennium is no higher than its level during the mid-1970s and certainly far behind that of comparable countries.

4
Turkey: Secularism with an Asiatic Connotation

The military and the state

The role of the military in Turkish history is perhaps more profound than its role in the history of any other nation. In essence, the history of Turkey is marked by wars and conquests. Turkey emerged in the region as an army before it became a nation; as Lybyer (1913) argues, the Ottoman Empire emerged as an army before it was any thing else, and modern Turkey was also created after the demise of the Ottoman Empire by the direct action of the remnants of the Imperial army. After the collapse of the Ottoman Empire in 1918, a skilful and well-organised nationalist movement emerged, led mainly by army generals inspired by Mustafa Kemal, later Kemal Ataturk. Kemal was an army general who came out of the war with his reputation boosted. Though the process of transforming the Ottoman Empire started earlier during the 'Young Turks' movement, Kemal, initially in favour of radical change in the Sultanate, was eventually instrumental in abolishing it. The Republic of Turkey was proclaimed in October 1923 and the Islamic sultanate was ended. Kemal's aim was to establish a secular modern republic along the lines of some European countries. The relationship between the state and the military was well-defined and governed by the principle that the army must be kept loyal to the civilian government but not kept out of politics completely. The army, though it adopted the role gradually, regarded itself as the guardian of secularism as represented by Kemal's principles of modernity. Army officers who wished to take public posts were required to resign their posts and give up their uniform. This led to the establishment of a widely accepted tradition in Turkish politics for most of its modern history – that the top public posts such as the presidency and the premiership were occupied by generals in civilian uniforms.

Secularism was therefore imposed from above rather than evolving through a gradual socio-political process.

Despite the abolition of the Sultanate and Islamic Caliphate, Turkey remained economically backward, traditionalist and the vast majority of its people were peasantry living off the fruits of the land. The preservation of a secular state in a largely traditional society with a complex religious, ethnic and historical background was not easy. Mustafa Kemal recognised this paradox by keeping the army in the background as an instrument of power, as the guardian of secularism, and as the guarantor of stability without visible direct political involvement. Since that time, a complex relationship between the army and the civilian apparatus of the government has developed and this relationship has become the most important pillar of modern Turkey. To this day, the army prides itself on adhering to the Kemalist principle of it as the guardian of secularism.

As discussed earlier, secularism was imposed from above on a country which was still traditional and religious to a high degree. The complete separation between state and Islam has remained one of the contentious issues in the society. Consequently, the army-imposed secularism didn't lead to a thriving modern political society like that of Western European countries. Until 1945, the state was largely based on a single-party system, and the development of a pluralistic political system was effectively prevented from flourishing. As in both ancient Asiatic societies and modern dictatorial governments, the state considered itself above the fray of party politics and the narrow interests of individual classes in society. The ruling elite assumed the role of the guardian and the protector-defender of the nation and heads of the state were regarded as father figures to the nation. Until 1950, the regime that ruled Turkey was in effect similar to other military regimes in the Middle East. Up to the general election of 1950, the country was ruled by Kemal Ataturk's party – the Republican People's Party (PPR). The move towards a multi-party system was allowed by Ataturk's successor and close colleague, General Ismet Inönü, in 1946 when the Democratic Party was formally established on 7 January 1946. The latter won the election of May 1950 by a landslide. It captured 420 of the 487 seats in General Assembly.

The massive defeat of Ataturk's party was indicative of the general public's resentment of the totalitarian regime established in the aftermath of First World War and the desire for a pluralistic system of government. This and other democratic elections held in the country contradict the wisdom held by the Turkish army that the Turkish nation is incapable of exercising modern democracy, and that the presence of the army in the background was essential for the protection of the nation against internal and external threats. Indeed, after the PPR's defeat in the 1950 election, the army was not comfortable with allowing a non-Ataturk political party to rule the country. Hale (1994) argues that the army's opinions on the transition to a multilateral party system was divided. While some army generals approached Inönü and suggested that they should launch a coup to annul the result of the election, Inönü, himself a former army general, was adamant that the result of the election must be respected and that the army should keep out of politics.

It was in the late 1940s that an important change with regard to the relationship of the army with the government was introduced by legislative changes reducing the status of the Chief of General Staff. Under legislation passed in May 1949, the Chief of Staff was effectively made responsible to the Ministry of Defence rather than the Prime Minister. This change of hierarchy has, at least on paper, made Turkey compatible with other democratic countries. In reality, however, the moral authority of the army in the collective memory of the public is still far stronger than its formal status. This authority was gained through repeated intervention in the public domain. Jenkins (2001) argues that the informal authority of the army as an institution far exceeds that of any politician, including the Prime Minister.

The democratic government was successful in its early years. The liberal economic programme of the government resulted in higher economic growth and a visible improvement in the wellbeing of the population. This reinforced the government's popularity. However, the good fortune of the government didn't last long as the economy slowed down in the second half of the 1950s and inflation started to rise, eroding the rises in the standard of living gained in the first half of the decade. Civil strife and public discontent with the economic changes and the erosion of the standard of living led the government to declare martial law in Istanbul and Ankara. The army, which was watching the government as well as the public, took the opportunity to remove the democratically elected government in a coup on 27 May 1960. Prime Minster Menderes and his cabinet were arrested with all former Democratic Party MPs for violating the constitution. They were put on trial and Menderes was executed with two of his supporters, while President Bayar's death sentence was commuted to life imprisonment. This set a precedent in Turkish politics that the country could be ruled by a democratically elected government only with the approval of the army. The army subsequently suggested that the Turkish public was still too immature to rule itself; therefore, the presence of the army in the background as a guardian of secularism is an essential feature of Turkish politics.

The military justified the coup by referring to the need to prevent civil unrest and resolve the political impasse. Some experts argue that the democratic government's handling of civil unrest was a graver violation of the constitution than the military coup itself. The military also established its credentials as the guardian of the Kemalist state through the coup.

The military stuck to its promise and handed back the government to civilian rule after a year and a half. The new government, under strict political conditions, operated under the watchful eyes of the military. The old Kemalist RPP party, led by the veteran Ismet Inönü, headed the new government despite its massive defeat in the previous general election. The next ten years, before a second military coup in March 1971, was a period of economic and social instability. Ultra-right and left-wing political organisations pursued supremacy of the streets of the main cities using violence, political assassinations and intimidation. Universities became battlegrounds for political settlement and armed robberies became commonplace and fuelled further violence. By the end of the 1960s, the economy was also hard hit by continued industrial disputes and trade union demonstrations. At the beginning of the 1970s, the second democratically elected government seemed unable to exert the state's control over political developments in the country. Turkey was gradually sliding towards anarchy and political chaos. On 12 March 1971, the military, for the second time, decided to intervene and end the political instability. Though the analysis of the background of the coup is beyond the scope of this book, the main justification of the coup leaders for the removal of a democratically elected government from power (Demirel's Justice Party was elected to office in October 1969) was that the civilian government was unable to control political and social forces and therefore it was the duty of the military to intervene and preserve the Turkish Republic.

Indirect military rule lasted about three years until the October 1973 election which brought back the RPP to power. The new government was faced with mounting economic and political difficulties. Despite a high economic growth rate during 1973–7, the economy was facing new challenges. As an oil importer, the country was facing a high energy bill as a result of the quadrupling of oil prices. Inflation rates increased and the devaluation of the country's currency, the lira, became inevitable. By 1980, the inflation rate rose to over 100 per cent and the country's balance of payments deficit increased to over $3bn. To deal with the economic problems, the government resorted to foreign borrowing and by the end of the decade the country's foreign debt rose to above $19bn from below $2bn in 1970.

The economic crisis was exacerbated by a rise in political instability. Between 1973 and 1980 there were ten successive governments. Serious political violence fuelled by ideological, religious and ethnic conflicts erupted to an unprecedented level. Unlike previous incidents of political and social instability, the 1970s civil unrest brought out the Kurdish as well as the minority Alevis (15 per cent of the population belongs to the Shi'ite sect called Alevis) problems to the forefront of Turkish politics. By the beginning of the 1980s, there was a fear that the country may be slipping down the path of Lebanon into a state of civil war. In that situation, a military intervention to restore stability became inevitable. Therefore, after almost seven years of civilian rule, the military stepped in on 12 September 1980 and removed the democratically elected government from power.

Unlike the previous military rule, the 1980s military-backed government lasted three years and three months; much longer than the previous military regimes. The military, however, restored order and ended political violence at a huge cost. According to Amnesty International (1980), the London-based human-rights organisation, more than half a million people were arrested and the vast majority of them were tortured while hundreds of others were executed. The military government also adopted brutal political repression. Virtually all trade unions and professional associations were prohibited, a wide range of literature, newspapers and films were banned and 14,000 people were stripped of their citizenship. As a member of NATO, the US approved the military coup and covertly supported the actions of the government. Nonetheless, unlike many military coup cases in Latin American countries, the leaders of the 1980 coup in Turkey were never held accountable by subsequent civilian governments for the atrocities or human-rights abuses they committed. Rather, they enjoyed happy retirements in the glow of military honour. Some of them are still alive and well to this day.

The military handover of the government to an elected civilian government was carefully choreographed after a constitutional change and the banning of undesirable political parties. In the late 1983 election, the Motherland Party led by Turgut Özal was elected only after its two main rivals, the True Path Party and the Social Democracy Party (SDP), were arbitrarily excluded from the race by the military.

The 1980s witnessed the rise of the ethnic Kurdish nationalist movement largely led by the Kurdistan Workers' Party (PKK) and the resurgence of Islamic-leaning political parties. These two tendencies were high on the military's list of threats facing the nation. Subsequently, the military waged a campaign widely known as the 'dirty war' against the Kurds in the southeast of the country in which over 35,000 people were killed and more than 3,000 villages were razed to the ground. During this war, the military enjoyed unparalleled support from the civilian government as well as from the Turkish public in large.

The fourth important military direct intervention in political life was in fact not brought about by political instability but was caused by the rise of political Islam. Since the 1980s and because of various internal and external factors, including the global resurgence of political Islam and the ideological vacuum left by the collapse of the Soviet Union, electoral support for Turkish Islamists started to become a real political force in the country. This formed a formidable threat to the principles of Kemalist secularism. The pro-Islamic Welfare Party (WP) rose to prominence in 1994, after winning local elections, and seriously alarmed the military. Through various public speeches and interviews, the top military brass, including Kenan Evren, the then President, warned that the military would not hesitate to take measures deemed necessary to defend secularism against the rise of 'reactionary tendencies'. However, despite the military's effort to prevent the Islamists coming to power, Necmettin Erbakan, the chairman of the WP, became the first avowedly Islamist Prime Minister in June 1996.

The Islamist government remained in power for one year during which its relationship with the military deteriorated. On the one hand, the government sought to introduce Islamic codes of conduct into public life, on the other hand, the military sought to undermine Islamic ideology and to some degree ignore the legitimacy of the government. For instance, Jenkins (2001) reports that in May 1997 when the military launched a cross-border operation to strike at PKK bases in Northern Iraq, it informed the press before notifying the government. The coalition government led by Necmettin Erbakan finally resigned on 18 June and was replaced by a tripartite coalition from the Mother Party (MP), the Democratic Left Party (DLP) and the Democratic Turkey Party (DTP).

Yet, although the military succeeded in removing the Islamic-led government from power in 1997 by political pressure rather than direct military intervention, the support for a political Islam didn't dissipate completely. There is a long political tradition in Turkey of banned political parties being reincarnated in other forms with different names.

Indeed, the election and re-election of the Justice and Development Party (AKP) in 2002 and 2007 and its emphasis on the revival of Islam brought back the dilemmas of the 1990s to the political scene. The current political turmoil facing the government after the country's high court decision to ban the ruling party is a serious impasse that may lead to another political intervention by the military, though it may take a completely different form from its previous interventions.

The perceived security threats to the country

As discussed earlier, the military in Turkey enjoys unparalleled power that the civilian government is not permitted to compete with. Indeed, the implicit power that the military has acquired and practised has always overshadowed civilian governments. This power is enshrined in the constitution of the country. As Jenkins (2001) states, the Turkish Armed Forces Internal Service Directive is quite explicit about the internal and external role of the military. Article 85/1 of the directive states: 'It is the duty of the Turkish Armed Forces to protect the Turkish homeland and the republic, by arms when necessary, against internal and external threats' (Jenkins 2001, p. 45).

The military also has a strong presence on the National Security Council, with five of its members coming from the army. It also has a strong say in the drafting of the National Security Policy Document (NSPD) which periodically defines the internal and external threats to the country and sets the guidelines for security policies. Turkish military expenditure is driven by NATO commitments and the perceived internal and external threats to the country. On the external front, Greece stands as an immediate military threat. Though the investigation of the history of the conflict between the two countries is beyond the scope of this book, a brief overview of the hostility may be useful here. After 1923, the two countries enjoyed a period of good relationship governed by mutual respect for each other's sovereignty. Both countries joined NATO in 1952 and participated in the American-led Korean War in 1952. The relationship, however, was brought under considerable strain over the Greco-Turkish conflict in Cyprus. In the summer of 1974, a Greek-inspired coup in Cyprus led to a Turkish invasion of the northern part of the island. Turkey still holds about 40 per cent of the island's territory and 17 per cent of the population live in Northern Cyprus. Apart from the conflict over Cyprus, both countries have deep disagreements over the Aegean territorial space and continental shelf rights.

Scholars are divided over the implications of the Greco-Turkish conflict for military expenditure in both countries. Bauer (1999) offers a comprehensive review of literature on the conflict and concludes that there has been a certain level of arms race between the two countries since 1950 but the race was ended somewhere in the mid or late 1980s.

The other perceived external threats come from other neighbouring countries. The Turkish relationship with Iran, Iraq, Syria and the former Soviet republics of Central Asia has been acrimonious over a variety of different issues; some, as in the case of Syria, resulted in direct military confrontation in the late 1990s.

Internal threats, as specified by the aforementioned NSPD, come from fundamentalism, particularly the rise of Islamic fundamentalism, separatism represented by the Kurdish movement's aspiration for self-determination, and also organised crime.

It is obviously very difficult to separate the extent of the weight of each threat factor on the military expenditure of the country, but it is quite clear that the inability of the country to resolve its domestic and external problems over time has created an uneasy and sometimes edgy relationship with its neighbouring countries. Similarly, on the internal front, the inability of successive governments to resolve the Kurdish issue democratically has created a divided nation.

Apart from the perceived internal and external threats' implications for military expenditure, the army's political influence internally and externally necessitates a certain level of expenditure that maintains the prestige of the army as a reasonably well-paid and maintained important institution. Keeping this prestige means that the officer corps, which numbered 104,500 at the beginning of 2000, are reasonably well-paid and fed. Jenkins (2001) argues that the salaries of Turkish officers are slightly higher than those in the civilian service but considerably lower than salary levels in the private sector. It is also imperative to mention that the Turkish army numbered around 789,000 at the end of 1999. This means that 12.2 persons per thousand people are in the armed forces. This ratio is about three times the average world ratio during the same period (WMEAT 2003, Table 4.1). In addition to its opportunity costs, there is no doubt that maintaining such a big army requires enormous amount of resources in a country that is still regarded as a developing country.

The state of the economy

Turkey is an emerging middle-income country which has many features of a developing country. Since the 1970s, similarly to many other developing countries which were on the path of industrialisation, the Turkish economy has undergone tremendous structural changes. In the 1970s, the share of agriculture in the GDP of the country was relatively high (See Figure 4.1) and the majority of people were engaged in agricultural production. The contribution of the industrial sector was typically modest. Figure 4.1 also shows that currently the overall picture of the structure of the economy is similar to that of an industrial country. The contribution of the industrial sector to the economy had been rising steadily and had overtaken that of agriculture by the mid-1980s. By the beginning of the millennium, the contribution of the service sector to the economy had become greater than the combined contribution of the agricultural and industrial sectors. However, this picture could be

Table 4.1 Average GDP growth in Turkey and other regions, selected years, 1970–2005 (%)

	1970–9	1980–9	1990–9	2000–5
Turkey	4.7	4.1	3.9	5.1
MENA	5.97	2.21	4.30	4.50
Latin America	5.71	1.80	2.90	3.70
Sub-Saharan Africa	4.07	2.18	2.04	4.32
South Asia	3.60	5.70	5.38	7.36
OECD	3.71	2.95	2.48	2.32

Source: Calculated from World Bank, *World Development Indicators* (April 2008).

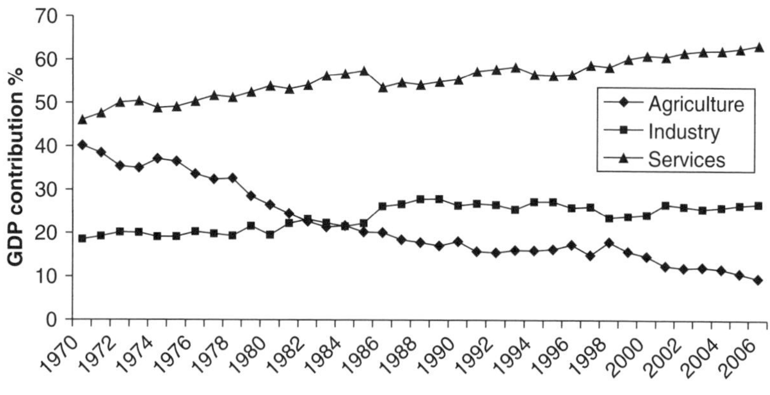

Figure 4.1 Sectorial distribution of GDP in Turkey, 1970–2007
Source: Calculated from World Bank, *World Development Indicators* (April 2008).

deceptive as the percentage of the labour force engaged in agriculture is still relatively very high. By the end of the millennium, more than 40 per cent of the labour force was still engaged in agricultural production, indicating the low productivity of the agricultural sector and the low absorption capacity of the other two sectors for the surplus labour force from the rural economy.

The economy's average annual GDP growth rate for the period 1970–2006 was 4.4 per cent, which is slightly higher than the average annual GDP growth rate of the Middle East and North African region, which was 4.15 per cent for the same period. However, this economic growth rate has varied significantly from one period to another. Figure 4.2 indicates that the economic growth of the country has been far from smooth. Indeed, the economy has experienced a decline in four different sub-periods. Utkulu (2001) argues that the economic decline experienced during the last half of the 1970s was largely due to collapse of the state intervention policy which subsequently led to political turmoil as well as an economic deterioration. High rates of inflation which were coupled with high foreign borrowing to deal with the balance of payments deficit experienced as a result of oil-price rises led to an external debt crisis by the end of 1978.

The turning point in the economy that was experienced during the 1980s was mainly due to the adoption of a new economic policy that the IMF approved and supported. The country adopted an outward-oriented and market-based policy, effectively reversing the previous state interventionist and inward import-substitution policy. During the 1980s and unlike many other developing countries, the average annual economic growth rate of the country was 5.23 per cent. As Figure 4.1 shows, the 1980s also witnessed another fundamental change in the structure of the economy, that is, the rise of the industrial sector's share of GDP above the contribution of the agricultural sector. It is worth mentioning that the outward-oriented policy of the government, which was associated with export support programmes and the devaluation of the Turkish lira, led to an unprecedented export growth. This positive situation, however, did not last long and by the beginning of the 1990s and the eruption of the first Gulf crisis, the economic growth rate slowed down to a mere 0.9 per cent in 1990. The 1990s were the most volatile economic period in the history of the economy. A high economic growth rate for a few years was followed by a recession. By 2002 the economy had experienced three big falls. The worst was during 2001 when the economy shrunk by 7.5 per cent.

The effect of the turmoil in the economic sphere on the average standard of living in the country was significant. Figure 4.3 shows that per capita GDP deterioration continued from 1977 until 1981. Indeed, the annual average growth rate of per capita income during the 1977–86 period was less than 1.0 per cent. This period also witnessed the highest rate of inflation, which reached 110 per cent in 1980.

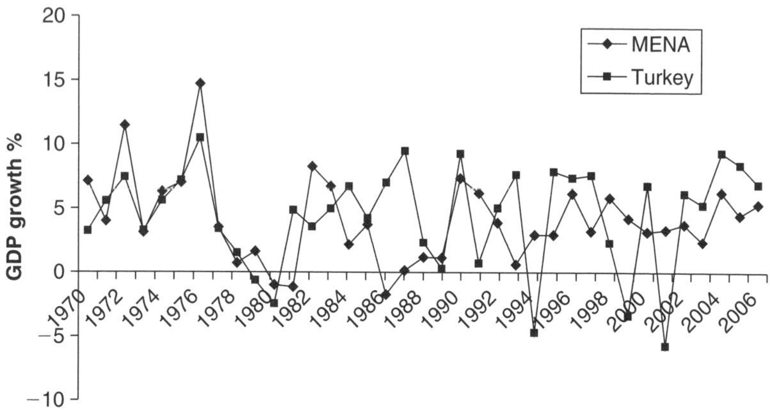

Figure 4.2 GDP growth in Turkey and the MENA region, 1970–2006
Source: Calculated from World Bank, *World Development Indicators* (April 2008).

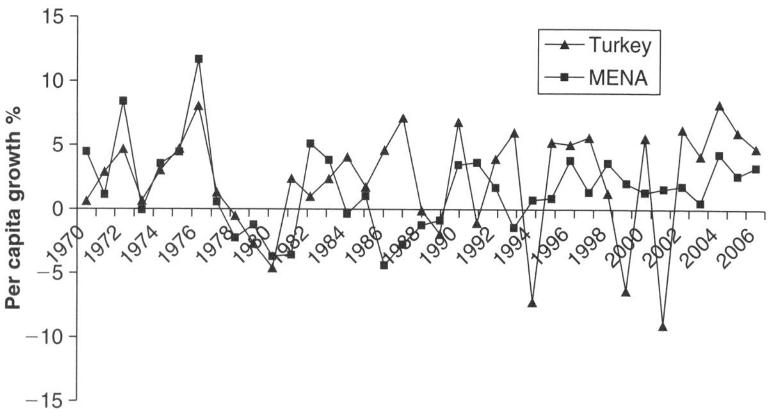

Figure 4.3 GDP per capita growth in Turkey and the MENA region, 1970–2006
Source: Calculated from World Bank, *World Development Indicators* (April 2008).

During the 1990s, per capita GDP growth was also abysmal. As was mentioned earlier, this was the result of frequent and relatively large fluctuations in economic growth. In fact, per capita income growth was a mere 1.59 per cent during that decade.

Another important characteristic of the economy is the heavy reliance on external debt for economic growth. An important reason for this is the structural problem of the country. Data shows that average national savings have consistently been below the developing countries saving rate of 22 per cent (Utkulu 2001). Subsequently, foreign sources of funds for investment have augmented domestic sources. In addition to this, the state has developed an inclination towards resorting to foreign debt to deal with economic and financial difficulties. Since the first stabilisation policies of the late 1970s and early 1980s, Turkey has enjoyed favourable relationships with the IMF and the World Bank. Öniş (1991) cites several reasons for this; firstly, the strategic importance of Turkey as an important member of the NATO alliance. Secondly, the Turkish financial crisis of the late 1970s preceded the Latin American countries' debt crisis and the IMF and the World Bank intended to make Turkey a case example for other countries. There is no doubt, however, that the economic turmoil of the late 1970s had the potential to destabilise the country to such an extent that the regional political situation could have been affected. Therefore, Turkey received five successive structural adjustment loans from the World Bank, regarded as a record number by World Bank standards. Though the assessment of the effectiveness of the foreign debt for economic growth and the successful dealing with economic and financial crisis in the country is beyond the scope of this study, data from Global Development Finance (April 2008) show that reliance on foreign debt has become an important characteristic of the economy. From a mere $2.745bn in 1970, the foreign debt of the country increased to $32.934bn in 1986, which amounts to a 12-fold increase. By the beginning of 1990, the country's debt had escalated to about $50bn. This figure increased to over $100bn by 1999 and by 2006 it reached an unprecedented level of $207.854bn.

Military expenditure

As discussed earlier, the military in Turkey has acquired a strong domestic political and social status through its self-appointment as the guardian of secularism represented by Kemal Ataturk's vision of modernity. The military indeed practised its power in the past repeatedly through direct and indirect political intervention in the government's affairs. This self-appointment has enormous socio-economic implications for the development of modern Turkey. Khilji (2005) argues that the repeated military intervention in political and social affairs of the country has effectively weakened the country's political institutions and strengthened the military's influence on domestic and foreign policy. The operations of civil institutions, such as parliament, the civilian government, educational and other social institutions are overshadowed by the presence of the watchful eyes of the military. They are constantly scrutinised on the basis of the military's criteria of secularism and they never feel free to operate according to their interpretation of the constitution or their formulation of secularism. On the other hand, the strong influence of the military on allocation of resources has in effect secured its own control over the level of military spending. Jenkins (2001) asserts that the military exercises almost total control over defence and defence procurement. The Turkish General Staff (TGS) has complete freedom to decide how funds are spent and when the government presents its budgetary proposal to the parliament, defence spending is the one item which even the opposition does not dare to challenge. In reality, military expenditure as a percentage of GDP has remained relatively stable despite the periodic economic turmoil that the country has experienced since the late 1970s. Figure 4.6 depicts the percentage growth of GDP and military expenditure as a percentage of GDP since the 1970s until 2006. It shows that military expenditure as a percentage of GDP has on average been above 4 per cent for three decades, although it experienced a decline during the 1990s and the beginning of the year 2000. This stability of military expenditure in spite of the political and economic difficulties of the country is a manifestation of the implicit and explicit power of the military over resource allocation between different alternatives in the country. Such exclusive power is normally only held in countries which are under military dictatorship.

The impact of military expenditure, however, has been investigated in several empirical papers, with a variety of conclusions drawn. Sezgin (1997) and Özsoy (2000) have found a positive and statistically significant overall effect of the Turkish military sector on Turkish economic growth for the period 1949–1993. Both papers have been criticised by Bauer (2001) on the grounds that models employed in those papers are inherently designed to find positive contributions of military expenditure to economic growth. In both papers *physical investment* and *human capital* effects on economic growth turned out to be statistically insignificant. Another shortcoming of both studies is that they have taken the impact of military expenditure out of the political economy context

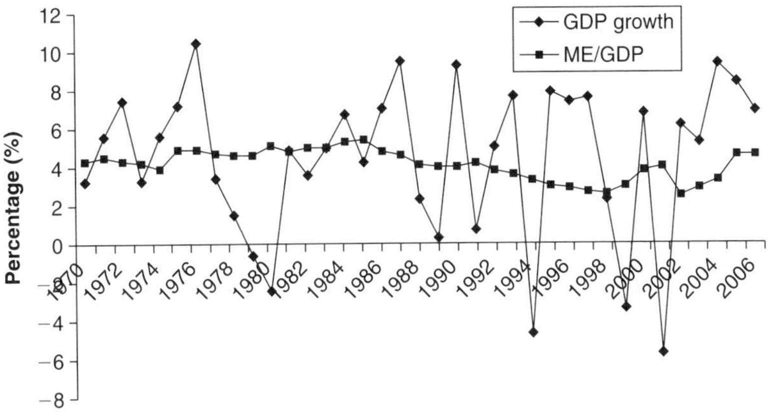

Figure 4.4 GDP growth and military expenditure (ME) as a percentage of GDP in Turkey, 1970–2006

Sources: GDP growth rates are calculated from World Bank, *World Development Indicators* (April 2008) and ME/GDP data are from SIPR, *Yearbooks* (various issues).

and have exclusively narrowed it down to economic growth. In another study, Özmucur (1996) has investigated the impacts of military expenditure from a different approach. The paper looks at the peace dividend of reducing military expenditure in the country. The conclusion of the paper is that there is a negative relationship between defence expenditure and expenditure on health and education. In another empirical study, Karagol (2005) has found that there is a long-run relationship between external debt and military expenditure in Turkey. Military expenditure has been found to have had a positive effect on external debt in the 1955–2000 period.

Military expenditure during the 1970s

In the 1970s Turkey witnessed two important political events with various long and short-term consequences; the first was the second military coup on 12 March 1971 which removed the civilian government from power and established the military's credentials as a proverbial sword of Damocles over the head of future civilian governments. This second military coup established the pattern and gave out a clear message to politicians that the military is always ready to intervene in politics. As discussed earlier, this indirect military rule lasted about three years until the October 1973 election which brought the RPP into power again.

The second important event was the eruption of the conflict with Greece over Cyprus in 1974 and its subsequent implications for military expenditure and the souring relationship of Turkey with the US. As mentioned earlier, on 20 July 1974 Turkey invaded Cyprus to protect the Turkish minority and it still occupies 40 per cent of the island to this day. As a result, the US suspended all its military aid to Turkey on 18 December 1974. The embargo lasted until 1978 but left a big rift in NATO's internal cohesion as both Greece and Turkey were members of the organisation. Table 4.2 shows that the event led to a rise in military expenditure to $2.980bn from $1.894bn, an increase of 57 per cent. The other impact of the invasion and subsequent US embargo was that Turkey started diversifying away from relying solely on the US as its major arms supplier and it also started strengthening its endogenous arms industry sector. The table also shows that there is little or no relationship between the growth rate of GDP and military expenditure. With the exception of the last two years in the decade, the two rates have changed independently of each other. Though, as emphasised previously, the data should only be taken as an indicator of the costs of military expenditure, the table shows that the military expenditure of the country amounted to $23.367bn during the 1970s. The table also shows that Turkey on average has spent about 4.5 per cent of its GDP on the military.

Table 4.2 Turkish military expenditure 1970–9, in $m, at 1978 prices and exchange rates

Year	Defence budget ($m)	Percentage increase	GDP growth rate (%)	ME as a percentage of GDP
1970	1,448	–	3.3	4.3
1971	1,655	14.3	5.6	4.5
1972	1,683	2.0	7.4	4.3
1973	1,880	11.7	3.3	4.2
1974	1,894	0.0	5.6	3.9
1975	2,980	57.3	7.2	4.9
1976	3,420	14.8	10.5	4.9
1977	3,320	–2.9	3.4	4.7
1978	2,728	–17.8	1.5	4.6
1979	2,368	–13.2	–0.6	4.6
1970–9	23,367			

Sources: SIPRI, *Yearbook* (1980, 1981); World Bank, *World Development Indicators* (April 2008).

Military expenditure during the 1980s

The 1980s also witnessed two important political events, though with different short and long-term consequences for the socio-political conditions in the country. The first was the military coup on 12 September 1980. Though the military's pretext for the coup was to curb the political violence that spread during the late 1970s, the coup came at the right time to avert a region-wide political change that might have exacerbated the already volatile situation after the 1979 Islamic Revolution in Iran. As a member of NATO and a close ally of the US, Turkey's actions during the coup may not have been sanctioned by the US administration but they were certainly not disapproved of. After the coup, the army unleashed a systematic campaign of political suppression against political groups of both the right and the left of the political spectrum. The widespread human-rights abuses committed by the army soured the political relationship between Turkey and some European countries but didn't affect its relationship with the US. In fact, as Dagi (1996) states, American economic and military aid to Turkey increased significantly in this period. It amounted to $453 million in 1981, $704 million in 1982 and $688 million in 1983, and the level of grants in US aid packages increased substantially.

The 1980s also witnessed the rise to prominence of the Kurdish political movement in the southeast of Turkey (Northern Kurdistan). The Kurdish Workers Party (PKK), a political organisation with a Marxist-Leninist leaning, emerged and took root during the civilian rule in the late 1970s. The PKK adopted a policy of self-determination for the Kurds in Turkey and took an active role in rural Kurdish areas. Sensing the likelihood of a crackdown after the military coup, the leadership of the PKK retreated to Syria and Lebanon to set up training camps for long-term guerrilla campaigns. As with other military responses to Kurdish self-rule aspirations, the military adopted brutal measures to deal with the issue. Subsequently, the PKK received the heaviest blow directed against allegedly subversive militant groups. Despite the heavy crackdown on political activities in the southeast of Turkey, the PKK came out not just unscathed but relatively stronger and far better organised than was expected. The military's collective punishment campaign against the Kurds effectively polarised Kurdish public opinion as well as the Kurdish political movement around PKK, strengthening the Kurdish cause as well as the PKK guerrilla campaign in the southeast. Subsequently, the southeast of Turkey was put under 'emergency rule' for decades.

To suppress the Kurdish movement, the military adopted two different military tactics, each with implications for the overall military expenditure of the country. The first was to implement counter-insurgency measures to reduce the areas regarded as a hotbed for PKK fighters. Among these measures, the military, from the mid-1980s, started burning, evacuating and destroying Kurdish villages, mainly along the borders with Iraq and Syria. According to Gabelnick (1999), and various other human-rights reports, in its campaign the military violated international human-rights and humanitarian law with its indiscriminate and disproportionate use of force. As a result of the campaign, and according to Filkins (2003), as many as 4,000 villages and hamlets were destroyed and hundreds of thousands of people were rendered homeless.

The second military tactic the military used to de-link PKK fighters from local support was the introduction of a village guard system. Akin to Peru's strategy against the Shining Path guerrilla movement, the military started to arm Kurdish villages to combat the PKK. The PKK responded to the policy with harsh measures against villages that cooperated with the government. The counter-measures adopted by the PKK were no less harsh than those adopted by the military in the region, and resulted in thousands of deaths on both sides leading to enormous social and economic consequences.

Though a full account of the human and social outcomes of the government's war against the PKK and the Kurds in general is beyond the scope of this book, it is essential to point out that the war against the PKK and the suppression of the Kurds have served as an excuse to suppress political freedom, press freedom and human-rights organisations. To this day, the Kurdish question in Turkey is far from resolved and the question indeed forms one of the most important legal and political obstacles against Turkey's membership of the European Union.

The economic and sociological implications of the war against the Kurds are immeasurable by conventional means. They include the immediate costs of the prolonged military campaign, the costs of the village guard system and operations, the opportunity costs of destroying up to 4,000 villages, and the displacement and resettlement costs of more than one million productive people. The long-term social dimension of the war is also colossal. The war and its continuation have left millions of people uprooted from their homeland and socially traumatised and psychologically scarred for years to come. These costs are either not directly measurable in monetary terms or not accounted for in the calculation of the military expenditure of the country. According to the US Central Intelligence Agency (CIA) *Factbook* for Turkey (1998), the military expenditure account in 1996 did not include about $7bn allocated to the government's counter-insurgency efforts.

Another aspect of the problem is the likely effects of the war on Turkey's external debt. As discussed earlier, Karagol (2005) has found that there was a long-run relationship between external debt and military expenditure in Turkey in the period 1955–2000. The logical conclusion is that the military's campaign against the Kurds in the southeast of the country is expected to have had an impact on the country's external debt. Data from the World Bank *Global Development Finance Report* for 2008 shows that by the beginning of the 1990s the country's external debt had reached $49.424bn from a $21.609bn in 1984. This amounts to a 128.72 per cent increase. Though it is difficult to measure the proportion of the external debt that may be attributed to military expenditure, nonetheless by 1990 the data indicates that the country's total external debt since the military's last coup in 1980 increased by about $30bn.

Table 4.3 shows the estimated military expenditure during the 1980s. There is every indication that the data do not take into account the aforementioned costs of the military suppression against the Kurds in the southeast of the country and the entailing increase of the debt burden of the country. The table also shows that the country has on average spent 4.71 per cent of its GDP on the military, which represents a slight increase from its level during the previous decade.

Table 4.3 Turkish military expenditure 1980–9, in $m, at 1988 prices and exchange rates

Year	**Defence budget ($m)**	**Percentage increase**	**GDP growth rate (%)**	**ME as percentage of GDP**
1980	1,876	–0.29	–2.5	5.1
1981	2,316	25.22	4.9	4.8
1982	2,528	–3.13	3.6	5.0
1983	2,393	–3.61	5.0	5.3
1984	2,325	–8.91	6.7	5.4
1985	2,467	10.50	4.2	5.3
1986	2,772	10.64	7.0	5.0
1987	2,647	9.24	9.5	4.9
1988	2,664	–7.31	2.1	3.0
1989	2,715	15.76	0.3	3.3
1980–89	24,703			

Sources: SIPRI, *Yearbook* (1990); World Bank, *World Development Indicators* (April 2008).

Military expenditure 1990–2006

The Kurdish insurrection continued throughout the 1990s and still remains a major security issue. However, the regional security picture has undergone a major change since the beginning of the 1990s. During the early 1990s, Iraq invaded Kuwait and was then ejected by a multinational force led by the US. Iraq was subsequently severely weakened militarily. The creation of the 'safe haven' through which the Kurdish minority in Iraq was granted UN protection led to further political developments that created another political and security concern for Turkey. After the creation of the 'safe haven', the Kurds quickly grasped the opportunity, conducted a general election in their region and established semi-independent self-rule for themselves. Though with little economic means, the creation of a self-ruled Kurdish government in part of Kurdistan had enormous ramifications for the rest of the Kurds in

Table 4.4 Turkish military expenditure 1990–2006, in $m, at 2005 prices and exchange rates

Year	Defence budget ($m)	Percentage increase	GDP growth rate (%)	ME as percentage of GDP
1990	10,129	–	9.3	2.0
1991	10,405	2.7	0.7	1.7
1992	10,956	5.3	5.0	1.4
1993	12,106	10.5	7.7	1.5
1994	11,839	2.2	–4.7	2.4
1995	12,162	2.7	7.9	1.8
1996	13,617	12.0	7.4	1.9
1997	14,187	4.2	7.6	2.1
1998	14,865	4.8	2.3	2.4
1999	16,414	10.4	–3.4	3.0
1990–9	126,680			
2000	15,885	–3.2	6.2	3.8
2001	14,562	–8.3	–5.3	4.0
2002	13,752	–5.6	6.2	2.5
2003	12,286	–10.7	5.3	2.9
2004	10,973	–10.7	9.4	3.3
2005	10,301	–6.1	8.4	4.6
2006	11,080	7.6	6.9	4.6
1990–2004	215,519			

Sources: SIPRI, *Military Expenditure Database* (2008); World Bank, *World Development Indicators* (April 2008).

other parts of Kurdistan. Fearing that the Kurdish experience in Northern Iraq would inspire its own Kurdish minority, Turkey became anxious about its security. On the other side, the PKK, exploiting the security vacuum on the border with Iraq, moved into Northern Iraq and started launching cross-border attacks on Turkish army and security forces.

Though the expected costs of the impact of the escalation of the conflict with the PKK is difficult to measure, Table 4.4, as an indicator of military expenditure, shows that, on average, Turkey spent about $12.678bn during 1990–2006 compared to $2.470bn during the 1980s. This is despite the fact that during this period Turkey has managed to forge a much better security agreement with Syria and Iraq and has signed a defence agreement with Israel. Therefore, with the exception of the PKK problem, the southern flank of Turkey has become relatively much more secure compared to the past two decades or so. It is also worth noting that looking at the growth of military expenditure and the economy during the period covered, the two growth rates hardly correlate. For instance, during 1994 and 1999, the economy experienced big downturns whereas military expenditure was positive and increasing. Contrary to this, as the economy was experiencing a healthy growth rate between 2000 and 2005 (except during 2001), military expenditure declined substantially.

Conclusion

The above analysis indicates that Turkey is facing a relatively low security risk from its neighbours. Though the hostility with Greece, another member of NATO, has in the past escalated to near confrontation, it has never been a major threat to the country. The country has also faced potential indirect threats from violence which has blighted its southern and eastern neighbours but they have posed little risk to the country's security. Indeed, most of the time, Turkey has enjoyed a relatively stable relationship with Iran, Iraq and Syria. The most dangerous and perhaps contentious security problem facing the country, and which it has not yet resolved, is the Kurdish nationalist movement in the southeast of its territory.

Despite this, as Table 4.5 indicates, Turkey remains one of the largest recipients of conventional weapons in the world. Though its rank has declined from first during 1991–5 to ninth during 2004, Turkey still spends a considerable amount of its resources on its military regardless of the general economic conditions facing it. According to WMEAT (2003), Turkey still has the sixth largest army in the world after China, the US,

Table 4.5 The ten largest recipients of major conventional weapons in the world, various periods, $m, at constant 1990 prices

Recipient	**1991–5**	**Rank order**	**1995–9**	**Rank order**	**2000–4**	**Rank order**
China	4,747	7	3,994	9	14,609	1
India	4,747	6	4,637	6	10,152	2
Greece	5,756	5	4,091	8	7,243	3
UAE	2,120	17	3,268	10	7,048	4
South Korea	3,774	11	6,011	4	3,884	5
Australia	–	–	–	–	3,461	6
Israel	4,293	8	2,903	11	3,457	7
Egypt	7,138	2	4,741	5	3,039	8
Turkey	8,096	1	6,461	3	2,945	9
Iran	–	–	–	–	2,572	10

Sources: SIPRI, *Yearbook* (1996, 2000, 2007).

India, North Korea and Russia. If Turkey can resolve its internal political problem with its Kurdish minority through non-military means and becomes a truly democratic country, the scope for reducing its military expenditure is enormous and the social and economic peace dividend would be immeasurable.

5
Iraq: The Unholy Marriage of Adversaries

The role of the military

The Ottoman Empire's rule over Iraq extended from the mid-16th century until the end of the First World War. A fertile land with two major rivers, the Euphrates and Tigris, it was regarded as a jewel in the crown of every Empire. Before the Ottomans, the area currently known as Iraq was the centre of the Abbasid Caliphate which thrived on taxation levied on trade and agriculture. The fame of the Abbasid receded gradually as its military might was weakened by a combination of internal and external factors which culminated in its demise at the hands of the Mongols in 1258. Iraq was conquered by the Ottomans in 1535 and until 1916, with the exception of a relatively brief period of Iranian Safavid rule between 1623 and 1638, Iraq remained an important part of the Ottoman Empire. However, during the Ottoman occupation Iraq had already lost its economic significance and reputation as the centre of Islamic studies, art and scholarly activities. Its population dwindled due to various invasions and diseases, its irrigation canal networks were ruined and city centres became dilapidated.

The Ottoman period left an everlasting effect on the country. The three *vilayets* or provinces (Baghdad, Basra and Mosul) comprising the current country were ruled centrally from Iraq for most of the time. The Turks relied on their army to subdue the predominantly nomadic population and collected taxes. In the late 19th century, the sons of tribal chieftains, notables and merchants were sent to Istanbul to study and later to join military academies. It was that group who, at the dusk of the Empire, became politically active and participated fervently in the formation of current Iraq and subsequently left their mark on the modern history of Iraq.

By the end of the First World War much of today's Iraq was occupied by Britain. On 25 April 1920, at the San Remo Conference in Italy, Iraq was formally made a mandate entrusted to Britain. Before the war, however, Britain was in touch with Arab nationalists such as the Sharif of Mecca, Hussein Bin Ali, who claimed to be a descendent of the family of the Prophet Muhammad. Hussein was encouraged and subsequently supported by Britain to lead the Arab Revolt against the Ottomans and was promised to be made king of an independent Arab state when the Ottomans were defeated. Hussein joined the British forces in 1916 and marched from Hejaz northward into Transjordan, Palestine and Syria. As the Ottomans were pushed northward, many army officers of the Ottoman army of Arab origin deserted the defeated army and joined the British and the Sharifian ragtag army. Amongst these were a group of Iraqi officers who either became politically active through their participation in the Young Turks' movement, which at the beginning of the century aspired to reform and modernise the Ottoman Empire, or were inspired by the Sharif's political aspiration towards an independent Arab state.

Because the Ottoman Empire followed the Sunni creed of Islam and was in a state of continuous hostility with Shi'ite Iran, the majority of, if not all, Ottoman Iraqi army officers were drawn from a Sunni background. Though the full details of how the British sidelined the Shi'ites in the south and the Kurds in the north is beyond the scope of this book, it is worth mentioning that Britain's reliance on ex-Ottoman Sunni army officers for the establishment and running of Iraq cemented the political future of the country and set the foundation for an unstable country.

Iraq became officially an independent country and joined the League of Nations in 1932, albeit after signing a treaty with Britain which gave the latter the control of Iraqi foreign policy. The treaty also included a clause promising mutual help in wartime and stipulating that in exchange of British aid, equipment and training of the Iraqi armed forces, the British were entitled to use all Iraqi facilities and assistance including railways, ports and airports in wartime. In addition, the British were permitted to lease two airbases in Iraq.

The use of the army in political suppression was advocated by senior Iraqi politicians even before the formal independence agreement with Britain. The army was first used against the Kurdish revolt during the 1930s. Though they were defeated by Kurdish tribal forces initially, they gained superiority with the support of the British Royal Air Force and occupied the Barzan region in 1931. The second major use of the Iraqi army was the suppression of the Assyrian uprising in 1933 during which

1,000 Assyrians were massacred by the Iraqi forces, which acted with impunity for the first time. They killed civilians, including women and children, and burned 79 villages in total. Since the Assyrians were considered as British proxies, the army units which participated in the suppression were treated as heroes on their return. This set a precedent in Iraqi history that gave the army the power to kill without being investigated or punished.

The Army's first intervention in politics came during 1936 when General Bakr Sidqi, the so-called 'hero' of the Assyrian campaign, seized power in a *coup d'état*. Though the coup leaders advocated an indirect army rule in the country, it started an era of repeated direct and indirect military interventions in politics. The coup also set another unprecedented pattern in Iraqi politics – the public's outpouring of sympathy and support for the army's actions. Just a few days after the coup, the public, mobilised by communists, intellectuals and trade unions expressed their complete support for the army through public demonstrations in major cities. This unholy marriage between crude public sympathy and the military's zeal to manipulate politics became a pattern, widely expressed during Qassim's era from 1958 to 1963.

The second military coup occurred in 1938 when Prime Minister Al-Madfa'i was forced to resign under the pressure from the military and Nuri Sa'id returned to power. However, the most serious army intervention occurred during the Rashid Ali coup in 1941. In collaboration with Amin Al-Husayni, the Mufti of Jerusalem who resided in Baghdad at the time, four prominent army colonels, namely Salah al-Din al-Dabagh, Fahmi Sa'id, Kamil Shabib and Mohmud Salman, formed a pan-Arab nationalist group which started intervening directly in the affairs of the government. They simply became the king-makers of Baghdad. After disagreements with the government in 1941, they forced the Prime Minister, Taha al-Hashimi, to resign and ordered Rashid Ali to form a government of National Defence. Unlike the previous army officers, the four colonels were pan-Arab nationalists who were not just seeking the independence of Iraq from Britain but the ultimate liberation of Syria and Palestine. They eventually sided with Germany and Italy against Britain and its allies. This led to the second British invasion of the country in 1941 and the eventual hanging of the four colonels. The coup, however, left a long-lasting legacy within the nationalist movement in Iraq. The four army officers who conspired against Britain were highly revered by the general public and later idolised by the Ba'ath Party which took power in 1963. Simon (2004) argues that the pan-Arab nationalists were influenced by the teachings of the German officers in the Ottoman military academies and inspired by the Prussian role in the unification of Germany. Accordingly, they admired the German Nazi party and its war against France and Britain. Though by nature, armies of all persuasions easily express tendencies towards brutality, the 1941 coup manifested the Iraq army's tendency towards fascism in its early stages of development.

The army continued to aspire for office, inspired by the Egyptians' successful coup in removing the monarchy in 1952. On 14 July 1958 the army overthrew the monarchy in Iraq and established a republic led by army generals. Abdul-Karim al-Qasim, who led the coup, had no clear social or political plan for his government. He often sided with one political group against another. At the beginning of his rule, influenced by the Communists, he took upon wider social goals such as land reform and political and press freedom, as well as advocating a conciliatory approach towards the Kurds. The army, as in many other developing countries, was designed and trained to fight an enemy but not to govern. Not very long after the coup, conflicts with the pan-Arab Ba'ath party, the communists and eventually the Kurds started to create an unmanageable situation. The government used the army to suppress the Kurdish revolt which erupted in September 1961.

The army in general was incapable of resolving political and social problems through democratic and peaceful means. It is also true that the country did not develop democratic civil institutions to contain and deal with such political and social problems. Therefore, the relative political freedom enjoyed after the coup gradually diminished. Qasim was eventually removed from power in February 1963 and executed by the army, which then brought to power the pan-Arab Ba'ath party for the first time. Not long after that another coup removed the Ba'athists from power and the army restored its grip on power again. This was followed by a period of relative calm until 1968, when the Ba'ath party came back to power again through a military coup led by sympathetic army generals. The 1968 coup marked the end of military coups in Iraq and ushered Iraq into a new era of continuous civil and military rancour. Eventually, the dictatorship of Saddam Hussein was established in 1979 and other social groups and classes were isolated from power. To make matters worse, Iraq restarted its war against the Kurds in 1974 after a four-year respite. It is worth mentioning that the nationalisation of the oil sector in 1973–4 and the quadrupling of oil prices during the early 1970s paved the way for the import of expensive weaponry and modernisation of the army on a broad scale. The consolidation of power in the hands of Saddam Hussein and the growing strength of the army at the end of the 1970s was a suitable condition for waging another war at a time when the Kurdish conflict had waned. As discussed in Chapter 3, Iraq invaded Iran in September 1980 to curb the zeal of the new Islamic regime in Iran and to negate the terms and conditions of the Algerian Accord signed in 1975 between the Shah of Iran and Saddam Hussein.

The devastating war with Iran lasted eight years during which more than one million people were killed in both countries, with immense economic costs. Though, as mentioned earlier, the war was eventually ended by Imam Khomeini's acceptance of the 'deadly poison' in 1988, Iraq claimed to have won it by not losing it. The end of the war, however, was not the end of a war footing for the Iraqis and the Iraqi army. The war was ended on 20 August 1988 when the Iranian side reluctantly signed a ceasefire agreement. Iraq came out of the war with a sense of jubilance, with more than one million men under arms, more than 5,000 tanks and artillery, a good stock of Scud missiles, a large air force and above all an extensive arsenal of chemical weapons. Only the Israel defence force matched such a force in the region.

During the war with Iran, Iraq also received widespread military, intelligence and political support from the US and many European countries. The West turned a blind eye to the Iraqi use of the internationally prohibited chemical and biological weapons in the war against the Kurds. This outright political and psychological support for the over-zealous Iraqi leaders endangered the whole region and was indeed a recipe for another regional war. Just two years later, on 2 August 1990, Iraq invaded oil-rich Kuwait and renewed its old claim over its sovereignty. The invasion led to potential serious consequences for the regional balance of power as well as for the security of the oil supply from the Gulf region. Firstly, if Iraq was to succeed in annexing Kuwait, the massive oil reserves and Iraq's relatively superior human resources could have been used to build a strong military power that would have surpassed that of Israel, endangering the existence of that state. The second potential outcome was that Iraq would be in a position to threaten the oil supply from the Gulf region. Lastly, the combined Iraqi and Kuwaiti crude oil reserves would have given Iraq enough leverage to destabilise the world oil supply if it had wished to do so. These strategic reasons led to a decisive response from the US and its allies. Iraq was subsequently ejected from Kuwait on 28 February 1991. The following 12 years saw UN sanctions against Iraq, which weakened Saddam Hussein's regime but didn't end it. It was only after the pacification and isolation of Iran that the Iraqi role as a balancing power to the zeal of the Iranian Islamic regime was no longer required and finally, in February 2003, albeit for the wrong reasons, the US invaded Iraq and overthrew Saddam Hussein's regime.

It is worth mentioning at this juncture that both Gulf wars are shrouded with much controversy and the US role in both wars is subject to a great deal of discussion which is beyond the scope of this book. It is important, however, to assert that the Iraqi army and its top brass were hardly responsible for the outbreak of the Iran-Iraq war, the invasion of Kuwait and the invasion of Iraq by the US. Nonetheless, the military adventures of Saddam Hussein were based upon the Iraqi military's capability, and they cost the country enormous amounts in economic and human resources, resources that could have been used for economic development had Iraq had different political institutions.

The perceived security threats to the country

As in many other countries of the region, the Iraqi army was built not as a response to a direct external threat to the country but as clear strategy for increasing the country's military might relative to its neighbours and also to keep the new country together. For Iraq, the prospect of an arms race with Iran influencing the relative strength of the army is plausible. It is also true that military rule gave the military the monopoly over resource allocation in the country and by virtue of this it drew a lion's share of the wealth of the country for itself. Fisher (1963) finds a common pattern in Middle East coups which is easily recognised in Iraqi military coups. One important characteristic of the military coups in Iraq was that they were mounted when popular dissatisfaction with the government caused an impasse and civilian and political institutions in the country were incapable of resolving it by peaceful means. It is also true that the civil and political institutions of the country were not developed enough to deal with social problems democratically. Though the analysis of the perceived reasons or the justifications of each military coup is an extensive task which is beyond the scope of this book, it is however clear that in most of the cases, the military coup leaders assigned political and social objectives to themselves rather than leaving them to civil institutions to resolve. For instance, in 1958, the military justified its coup by social objectives because the pro-British monarchical regime was not meeting the aspiration of the general population for economic and social development. The army took upon itself the role of the saviour of the nation. It initially adopted wide social and economic objectives such as land reform and improving standards of living through increasing spending on education and health services. In almost all cases, however, statements about the liberation of Palestine and anti-imperialist rhetoric provided an extra pretext for military coups.

Despite the fact that Iraq, at some points in time, had border disputes with Iran over navigation rights on the Shatt al Arab waterway, there is no doubt that in all cases military coups in Iraq did not come as a response to external threats to the country, because Iraq did not face any tangible threat from its neighbours. In any case, Iraq and Iraq came to a peaceful agreement in Algeria in 1975, albeit at the expense of the Kurds. Perhaps the only credible threat from Iran came from the new Islamic government of Iran after 1979, when the new regime adopted a regime change policy in Iraq. While the threat should not be regarded as a full justification of the outbreak of the war it nevertheless provided the political milieu for it.

The most important and continuous threat that the country has grappled with since its establishment has been its dealing with the internal Kurdish movement for self-determination. Britain effectively carved out Iraq from the Ottoman Empire at the end of the First World War with no consideration for the Kurdish aspiration for self-rule and the Kurds in Iraq have never been happy with or accepted Arab majority rule. Therefore, they frequently mounted small and widespread revolts against Britain and later against the Iraqi government. Immediately after the war, sporadic revolts by Kurdish tribes broke out. This continued well into the 1940s. The most serious and perhaps the most determined Kurdish revolt was the 1961 revolution which continued until 1975. The Kurds, however, continued to fight the Iraqi government, albeit on smaller scale, well into the late 1980s. The Iraqi government in its suppression of the Kurds used extreme brutality such as dirty wars of attrition, mass evacuations, chemical weapons, and eventually what human-rights groups recognise as genocide during the notorious Anfal campaigns at the end of the 1980s in which about 200,000 Kurdish civilians disappeared. Though a large share of later atrocities committed against the Kurds can be attributed to the Ba'ath regime, the brutal inclinations of the army were evident from the beginning of the formation of the Republic of Iraq, when the army generally acted with impunity. Earlier, during the Assyrian campaign and later during the later part of General Qasim's rule, the army clearly demonstrated its brutal credentials. This culminated in the army's destruction of 4,000 Kurdish villages and the evacuation of their inhabitants in the late 1980s and the subsequent disappearance of hundreds of thousands of Kurdish civilians.

The state of the economy

Since the military coup in 1958 Iraq has suffered from repeated state intervention and direction of the economy, high military expenditure and, above all, an almost continuous internal war against the Kurds, as well as three other major, devastating wars. Despite the country's plentiful oil reserves, reasonably well-developed human capital and the availability of adequate arable land and water, living conditions and economic development have remained at a miserable level. The International Monetary Fund (2003) reported that as a result of the political turmoil that the country has experienced, the GDP per capita is estimated to have dropped from over $3,600 in the early 1980s to between $770 and $1,000 in 2001. Throughout the period of military rule, monetary and fiscal policies were completely subordinated to political objectives. The removal of Saddam Hussein from power in 2003 by the US-led coalition ushered the country into a new era of sectarian conflicts, direct and indirect intervention by neighbouring countries, terrorism and political instability. The invasion also had profound implications for the infrastructure and industrial base of the country. The extreme hostility towards the previous regime led to widespread looting of government-owned industries and projects, sabotage and destruction of government departments and institutions, and a near complete disruption of the major economic activities in the country. Iraq has also inherited the past regime's heavy debts and war reparation obligations and is considered to be one of the most highly indebted countries in the world.

It is also important to mention here that Saddam Hussein's regime, which ruled the country for 35 years (1968–2003), reported little data about economic indicators to international organisations such as the World Bank, the IMF and various UN commissions. The lack of reliable data on the economic activities of the past three decades makes any reasonable economic analysis of the country's economy very difficult.

In common with many other oil-exporting countries, Iraq became increasingly dependent on its oil revenues. At the beginning of the 1970s, its oil production was just below 1.5 million barrels a day. The oil price increase of the 1970s, combined with the nationalisation of the oil sector, led to an unprecedented increase in the country's oil revenues. Subsequently, the government saw its future in the further expansion of the oil sector and therefore increased production and exports. By the end of 1970s, Iraq's oil exports peaked at 3.247 million barrels a day. Though this level of oil production was a result of the second increase in oil prices and the Islamic revolution in Iran, it marked a new turn in the country's history. At an average price of $12.70 a barrel compared with $1.674 a barrel less than a decade before, it was a blessing to Saddam Hussein who had just consolidated his power after making himself the president of the country and liquidating his opponents. Saddam Hussein, a man of undistinguished origins, was largely known for his thuggery and sadistic gangster background in the Ba'ath party. He found himself in control of a country with huge oil reserves and a production capacity of more than 3 million barrels a day. Table 5.1 shows that during 1980 Iraq's oil revenues reached a record $26,096 million. The remarkable economic paradox of this era is that the peak of the country's oil earnings coincided with an era of economic decline and political turmoil. Oil production and exports continued to fluctuate during the 1980s as the war with Iran initially disrupted production and exports. As the country's foreign exchange reserves quickly depleted, the country's current account balance plunged into deficit. The regime resorted to external sources of funding to cover the costs of the war. The US and European countries were eager to support and sustain Saddam Hussein's regime against a presumably more dangerous and ideologically driven Islamic regime in Iran. The regime therefore found it easy

Table 5.1 Iraqi oil export values and current account balance, 1970–91

Year	Oil exports (million barrels/day)	Value of oil exports ($m)	Current account balance ($m)
1970	1,496	914	–
1971	1,618	1,206	–
1972	1,436	1,027	547
1973	1,926	1,842	801
1974	1,849	6,534	2,618
1975	2,059	8,227	2,705
1976	2,241	9,201	2,495
1977	2,167	9,560	2,990
1978	2,384	10,913	4,087
1979	3,247	21,382	11,117
1980	2,482	26,096	15,565
1981	872	10,422	–2,790
1982	846	10,096	–4,313
1983	702	7,816	–1,253
1984	867	9,354	907
1985	1,085	10,685	1,581
1986	1,394	6,905	–3,040
1987	1,717	11,416	2,300
1988	2,095	10,952	–136
1989	2,260	14,500	2,846
1990	1,596	9,463	–90
1991	43	380	–

Source: OPEC, *Annual Statistical Bulletin* (1990, 1992).

to borrow from the Gulf States, which were also threatened by the revolutionary zeal of the Iranian Islamic regime. Oil production recovered in the second half of the 1980s but the current account continued to be shaky. The reported data show that in the last six years of the decade, the current account surplus amounted to an average $577 million compared with over $15,500 million when the war broke out with Iran.

The conventional wisdom on whether oil was a curse or a blessing to Iraq can be easily elucidated by looking at the importance of the oil sector in the country's overall export revenues and gross national product. Figure 5.1 exhibits the ratio of oil-export revenues to the country's total export revenues as well as the ratio of the country's oil revenue to GDP. Starting from less than 60 per cent at the beginning of the 1970s, the ratio of oil revenue to the country's total export revenues rocketed to about 100 per cent of the country's total export revenues by the mid-1980s. In the 1980s, the country became completely dependent on its oil exports as the only source of foreign exchange earnings. The ratio of oil revenues to the GDP of the country followed the path of oil prices. As oil prices increased oil revenues started to overshadow the rest of the economy. Starting from just above 20 per cent of the economy at the beginning of the 1970s, the ratio of oil revenue to the GDP of the country increased to 90 per cent of the whole economy during 1980. As the oil production and exports of the country were disrupted by the war and in the light the decline of other sectors of the economy, the contribution of oil revenues to GDP declined to about 27 per cent of GDP by the end of the decade.

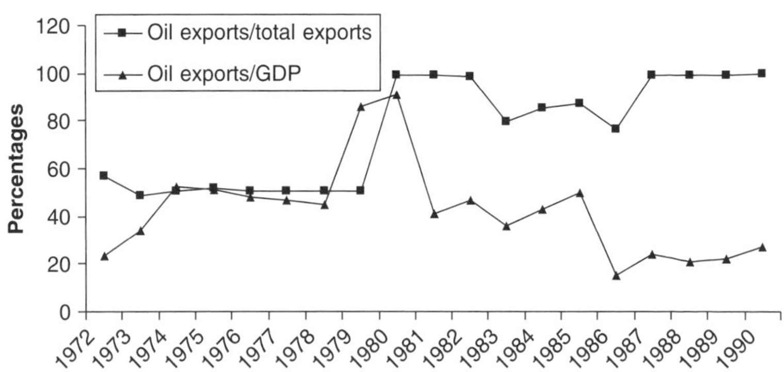

Figure 5.1 The ratio of the value of oil exports to total exports and GDP of Iraq, 1972–90
Source: Calculated from OPEC, *Annual Statistical Bulletin*, 1992.

The high oil revenues of the 1970s were widely used to lubricate the apparatus of a dictatorial regime and later to fuel the perverted personal ambitious of Saddam Hussein – with disastrous consequences for the country. Increases in oil revenues, therefore, could truly be considered as a missed opportunity for the country. Table 5.2 shows the sectoral distribution of GDP of the country. It could be easily inferred that during the period of high oil prices and oil revenues, the structure of the economy did not move towards industrialisation and economic development. In fact, as the table indicates, the share of total manufacturing declined from 57 per cent during 1975 to 33 per cent during 1988. It is also apparent that, contrary to the typical experience of newly industrialised developing countries, the contribution of agriculture to GDP doubled during this period rather than declining. Table 5.3 shows the estimate of growth rates of economic indicators of the country. It indicates that both public and private consumption plummeted, reversing the high consumption trends of the 1970s. This shows that the relative high oil revenues of the early 1980s, which were comparable to those of the late 1970s, were diverted to the war effort. The overall economic effects of the war were a decline of the economy by about 8 per cent in the first half of the 1980s. During this period manufacturing also shrunk by 7.8 per cent.

When the ceasefire with Iran was agreed, the economy of Iraq was in ruins and the standard of living of the majority of its citizens had severely deteriorated. The country's manufacturing sector was in decline and the country's infrastructure was extensively damaged. Public consumption was declining and inflation was increasing. Millions of foreign workers who were invited to the country to maintain basic services during the war, when more than one million of the country's indigenous workforce

Table 5.2 The sectorial distribution of GDP in Iraq, various years, 1975–88 (%)

	1975	1980	1981	1982	1984	1986	1988
Agriculture	8	5	9	10	13	15	16
Industry	57	66	37	32	34	27	33
Manufacturing	7	4	7	7	8	11	12
Construction	9	7	16	17	10	9	6
Trade	5	5	10	12	13	13	11
Transport & communication	5	4	7	7	5	7	7
Other activities	17	13	24	24	28	32	29

Source: UN (1991).

Table 5.3 Average growth rates of selected economic indicators, 1970–89 (%)

	1970–80	1980–5	1985–9
GDP	11.7	–8.1	–1.7
Private consumption	13.6	–1.3	–4.4
Gross fixed investment	27.6	–0.3	–1.5
Exports of goods & services	4.4	–8.8	–1.1
Imports of goods & services	22.5	–8.2	–2.9
Agriculture	1.4	6.3	–6.7
Industry	10.2	–7.3	11.4
Manufacturing	13.4	0.3	–3.1
Construction	28.4	–7.8	–16.2
Domestic trade	16.8	1.3	–10.8
Transport & communication	19.9	–12.4	1.8

Source: UN (1991).

were engaged in the war effort, became an economic burden. Iraq was also burdened by a massive amount of debt accrued during the war. Some of the debt which was owed to the Gulf States ($40bn) was later disputed by Saddam Hussein's regime as being economic assistance rather than loans. Iraq also owed $35bn to Western European countries and a further $11bn to the former Soviet Union. After the war, unfortunately, as Alnasrawi (1994) argues, Saddam Hussein's regime did not seem to be bothered with the immediate and overriding problems of the economy. Instead, the regime focused on its military-industrial complex, producing a wide array of conventional and chemical and biological weapons. Indeed, the regime's resolve to strengthen its military and military-industrial capability was well manifested by the amalgamation of the Ministry of Industry and the Ministry of Industrialisation Organisation into a single ministry which was called the Ministry of Military Industrialisation. This indeed was not just the final nail in the coffin of economic development; it revealed the intention of the regime to further engage the country in other wars with its neighbours. Within less than two years of the end of the war with Iran, the regime plunged the country into another serious conflict by invading Kuwait in August 1990. The following 12 years of UN sanctions against Iraq and the linking the country's oil exports to food imports under Oil-For-Food programme of the UN brought the whole country to its knees. The story of those 12 years is a catalogue of deprivation, abject poverty, human degradation and the breakdown of the fabric of the society. It is no wonder that after the invasion of the country by the US-led coalition in 2003, the ensuing chaos claimed more lives than the invasion itself.

The invasion and subsequent formal occupation have now halted the economic decline that Iraq suffered from over the past two decades. Oil production and exports rose to 2.183 million barrels per day in 2007 and per capita income reached $1,935. This can be considered remarkable compared with the economic decline of the 1990s but it is still far lower than the levels of the late 1970s. Despite this, the core ingredient that Iraq is lacking is the political stability essential to economic development. The invasion did not only get rid of a notorious regime but it also lifted the lid on a complex pot of non-homogenous sects and nationalities. These different sects and nationalities, mainly Shi'ite and Sunni Arabs and Kurds, were artificially joined together by Britain at the end of the Second World War and this was maintained by successive oppressive and dictatorial central governments in Baghdad. Whether or not some reasonable political harmony between these different groups can be achieved is a matter for the future to tell; what is essential to emphasise is that without such political and social stability, economic development is in peril.

Military expenditure

Since the military coup of 1958 (which many Iraqis regard as the 1958 Revolution), there has been a tendency to spend more and more on the army and strengthen the role of the army in the country. Since September 1961, the Iraqi government has been at war with its Kurdish minority at various degrees of intensity. The war continued until the 1970s when a truce was agreed between the Ba'ath party, which came to power in 1968, and the Kurdish movement. The agreement is widely known as the Manifesto of 11 March 1970. The truce provided the rather weak central government some breathing space to consolidate its grip on political power and the army. The government's failure to implement the Manifesto and its deliberate efforts to change the demographic composition of Kirkuk and other disputed regions of Kurdistan led to the resumption of hostilities with the Kurdish movement at the beginning of 1974. Perhaps these four years of relative political stability were the best opportunity for the government to build wider social and political alliances in the country. Unfortunately, as the following years' experience shows, the Ba'ath party's priority was not economic development. As noted earlier, the hostilities between the government and the Kurds were brought to an end after the signing of the Algerian Accord between Iraq and Iran in March 1975. According to the terms of the agreement, Iran ended its logistic and military support for the Kurds, which effectively terminated the hostilities in Kurdistan and paved the way for a swift demarcation of the disputed areas between Iran and Iraq. In return, the agreement constituted a formal Iraqi acquiescence to the Iranian dominance in the Gulf. Iraq subsequently granted Iran sovereignty over half of the Shatt al Arab waterway while Iran made no practical concession to Iraq.

During that period military expenditure and the size of the armed forces were both on the upswing. Though it is very difficult to come to definite conclusions about the reported data about military expenditure in Iraq, the data in Table 5.4 indicate that by 1975, military expenditure increased by more than 400 per cent compared to its level in 1970. Between 1975 and the outbreak of the war with Iran, Iraq, as Sluglett and Farouk-Sluglett (1990) argue, gradually loosened its ties with the socialist countries, moving into the general orbit of the West. Concurrently, Iraq started to diversify its sources of weapons imports away from East European countries. The first major order for Western arms dates to September 1976, when France agreed to sell between 60 and 80 Mirage F1 jet fighters, followed by an order for 200 French AMX 30 tanks in 1977. This move and the final breakup of the coalition with the Iraqi Communist party (The National Patriotic Front) paved the way for a much stronger relationship with the US and European countries. Though Iraq continued its anti-imperialist and Zionist rhetoric, there is strong evidence that the Ba'ath party did make its mind up about a positive long-term relationship with the West. The Iranian Islamic Revolution in 1979 polarised the regional political atmosphere in favour of the US and Western European countries. The anti-American and anti-Iraqi policy of the new Islamic regime in Iran united the efforts of the US and Iraq against this common enemy. The Iraqis' initial response to the Iranian revolution was cautious and officially positive. The Ba'ath party's regime was largely Sunni-based and the majority Shi'ite Arabs were largely distanced from political participation. The Iraqi government was apprehensive about the possibility that the Iranian Revolution may inspire its own Shi'ite majority. Though Iraq expressed a cordial reception to the Revolution, the new rulers of Iran didn't hide their hatred towards the Iraqi regime and insisted that the road to the liberation of Jerusalem went through Najaf and Karbala, the two Shi'ite holy cities in Iraq.

Before the full-blown war, small skirmishes between the two countries along their long border provided ample bases for further escalations. Blame and counter-blame were exchanged between the two regimes. The full details of the pre-war hostility between the two regimes are widely covered elsewhere.

Iraq commenced the war by bombing Iranian airbases to paralyse the Iranian air force. The Iraqis' pre-emptive attack was based on two premises; firstly, the Iranian armed forces were in disarray after the revolution's purge of the army of its pro-American top brass. Therefore, Iraq felt it could easily defeat the Iranian army on the battleground. Saddam Hussein thought that a quick and decisive blow to Iran would bring it back to its senses and that it would agree to a ceasefire. The second premise, as Sluglett (1990) argues, was the Ba'ath Party's overestimation of the degree to which the Iraqi Shi'ite population as a whole was in sympathy with, or prepared to support, the establishment of a theocratic regime in Iraq. In both cases, the Iraqi miscalculation misfired and led to disastrous outcomes. As the war continued, Iran didn't capitulate despite the overwhelming economic and military difficulties it was facing, and the Shi'ites in Iraq did not rise up against the Iraqi government in the way they had against the Shah in the Iranian Revolution. Unlike many other wars of comparable ferocity and destructive consequences, Iraq, the prime initiator and first mover in the war, had neither a clear strategy for the war and nor did it, as Karsh (1988) argues, pursue some wider ambition; instead Iraq was pushed into war as a result of increasing anxiety. Therefore, the Iraqis' ultimate aspiration was to contain the Iranian danger. This aspiration was also shared by the US, Western European countries and the Gulf States. It is quite plausible that Iraq would have been encouraged by the Gulf States' apprehension over Iranian ambitions to export the revolution to other countries, as well as by the US's hostility to the new regime. Although, as Kahdduri (1988) argues, Iraq was determined to go to war alone and win it single-handedly, its initial failure to bring the war to a rapid conclusion forced Saddam Hussein to revise his own regional strategy. After the first year of the war, and as the Gulf States were exposed to attacks from Iran, Iraq started claiming that it was waging the war on behalf of other Arab countries threatened by Iran and that it was the protector the eastern flank of the Arab nation.

The eight-year long war was beyond the imagination of the Iraqi leadership. The human toll of the war on both sides was estimated at 1.5 million people. The economic costs, however, were monumental. They included:

1. The potential losses to GDP as a result of losses incurred to the oil sector, the disruption to agricultural energy and industrial production, and collateral damage to infrastructure and production facilities. Alnasrawi (1994) estimates this to have been in the range of $91.4bn, although Mofid (1990) puts the figure at $67bn.

2. Disruption to oil exports to an estimated value of approximately $197.7bn.
3. $78.8bn of losses in foreign exchange reserves due to the loss of $33bn in original reserves plus accumulated interest over the duration of the war.
4. An estimated potential GNP loss of about $222.1bn, based on what was expected to be produced at pre-war GNP size and growth rates.

Therefore, the estimated total loss amounts to about $452.6bn. As Table 5.4 also indicates, direct military expenditure during the duration of the war amounted to about $178.2bn. However, these figures should be treated with utmost caution as there are wide discrepancies between SIPRI and WMEAT estimations. They should be considered only as trends rather than absolute figures.

The war also left Iraq with a huge external debt problem. As noted earlier, as the costs of the war mounted and Iraqi oil production was cut, Iraq started borrowing from the Gulf States and European and Russian creditors. By the end of the war, Iraq's total external borrowing was in the range of $90bn. It is also worth mentioning that the war left hundreds of thousands of wounded and handicapped people with huge potential costs that are difficult to measure and usually not accounted for in economic literature.

Table 5.4 Military expenditure, ME/GDP and armed forces in Iraq, 1970–90

	Military expenditures at current prices ($m)	**ME/GDP**	**Armed forces (thousands)**
1970	700	19.4	62
1975	3,100	22.5	82
1980	19,800	38.8	430
1981	24,600	66.0	390
1982	25,100	57.4	404
1983	25,300	59.5	434
1984	25,900	44.3	788
1985	19,000	37.9	788
1986	11,600	47.4	800
1987	14,000	43.1	900
1988	12,900	40.2	1,000
1989	12,900	32.0	1,000
Total 1980–9	191,100		

Sources: WMEAT (various); Alnasrawi (1994).

However, if the war with Iran was the result of folly and miscalculations by Saddam Hussein, the invasion of Kuwait was a premeditated decision by the Iraqi leadership as a whole. The war was begun with the economy of Iraq in ruins and the Iraqi people impoverished. The aim of the invasion was primarily economic; the Iraqi government made it abundantly clear that after the takeover of Kuwait, Iraq would be in a position to pay its debts back quickly and with combined Iraq-Kuwaiti oil reserves, Iraq would increase its production and export levels to a level sufficient to pay for its economic development. The miscalculation by Saddam Hussein in this case was his underestimation of the response of the US and Western European countries to his invasion. The response was indeed swift. Immediately after the invasion, the UN Security Council passed resolutions freezing Iraqi assets in the West, banned trade with Iraq and imposed mandatory sanctions and an embargo on both Iraq and occupied Kuwait. This effectively sealed the fate of the Ba'ath regime in Iraq. In the ensuing eviction of Iraq from Kuwait, known as the First Gulf War, Iraq's economic infrastructure was virtually destroyed by 42 days of aerial bombardment. Iraq was systematically and deliberately reduced to rubble. The Iraqi army was subsequently ejected from Kuwait in February 1991 and much of its armoury destroyed.

In a deliberate attempt to preserve Saddam Hussein's regime, the West spared the notorious Iraqi Republican Guard from destruction. In the immediate aftermath of the war, Iraq waged a war of retribution against the Kurds in the north and the Shi'ites in the south, both of whom had been encouraged to rebel against the government by the US. As a result, more than 100,000 lost their lives.

In the next 12 years, the Iraqi government was prevented from rebuilding its state apparatus by strict UN sanctions which prevented Iraq from exporting its oil. However, a certain level of exports was maintained under the UN Oil-For-Food programme.

Since the army and security forces were the regime's power base, Saddam Hussein's government continued to spend a relatively large amount of the country's scarce resources on their maintenance during the sanctions period. Since there are no reliable estimates of Iraq's military expenditures during that period, the figures in Table 5.5 should be treated with caution. The table indicates that Iraq continued to spend about a fifth of its GDP on military expenditure during the 1990s – one of the highest ratios in the world. In total, the country spent $53.286bn during the decade and maintained armed forces of 420,000. Cordesman (1999a) reveals that the army was paid a premium to ensure its loyalty. Though Iraq had to scale down its armed forces from over one million to

Table 5.5 Iraqi military expenditure, in current $m, 1990–9

	Military expenditure	ME/GDP	Armed forces (thousands)
1990	14,210	18.4	1,390
1991	8,776	17.5	475
1992	4,200	17.9	407
1993	3,530	18.5	407
1994	3,330	19.1	425
1995	3,600	19.7	415
1996	3,850	20.4	415
1997	3,930	21.0	415
1998	3,930	21.4	420
1999	3,930*	22.0	420
Total 1990–9	53,286		

Note: *1999 data is an estimate.
Sources: WMEAT (2001); Cordesman (1999a).

less than half a million during the 1990s, it certainly diverted resources away from the civilian economy and badly needed infrastructure in order to sustain a high level of military expenditure. However, there is no doubt that the sanctions reduced the military capability of the Iraqi army hugely. Iraq was prevented from importing weapons and its oil exports were severely limited by the UN Oil-For-Food programme.

Conclusion

The military in Iraq was the first established and perhaps the most powerful institution in the country between its formation by Britain in 1921 and its disbandment by the US after the 2003 invasion. The hard core of the army was initially formed from ex-Ottoman officers. From its inception, it had a love-and-hate attitude towards the state. With an exception of the Iraq's first decade, it either longed to overthrow the government or itself formed the government. History shows that the Iraqi military was mainly used as an instrument of power and largely for the sake of subduing internal dissent. As Al-Marashi and Salama (2008) note, the Iraqi military has hardly contributed to the stability of the country and has regularly interfered in its political development by either dictating the formation of a government or overthrowing it altogether. The military by and large mirrored the sectarian origin of the government; the military elite traditionally came from an Arab Sunni background. Out of the 27 top generals who participated in coups during military rule between 1958 and 1968 there was just one Shi'ite officer amongst them (Naji Talib), one half Kurd (Abd Al-Karim Qasim), one half Turkeman (Jalal Al-Awqati), and one half Turk (Ismail Arim); the remainder were Arab Sunnis. This tradition of officer recruitment was inherited from the Ottoman and British authorities who favoured, and indeed limited recruitment to, Arab Sunni.

Being an instrument of power, the military was allocated a large share of the country's resources and army officers were paid handsomely as a reward for their loyalty and service. With limited opportunities elsewhere, a career as an army officer was the road to the prestige and power that young males, particularly Sunnis, aspired to. There is no doubt that the top army officers were the most powerful men in the country and were kingmakers until the Ba'ath party *coup d'état* in 1968. The Ba'ath party attempted to pacify the military through 'Ba'athification' and purges. Throughout the party's reign, hundreds of top army officers were forcibly retired or sent to firing squads. In 1971, Saddam Hussein declared that 'with party methods there is no chance for anyone who disagrees with us to jump on a couple of tanks and overthrow the government' (Hirst 1971). This approach to the army sealed its fate and prevented it from coming to power again, despite various attempts during the 1980s and 1990s. However, this does not imply that the military was not paid handsomely or not lavished with perks and prestige in this Ba'athist period. In addition to the country's complex and well-established security forces, the army continued to be the instrument of oppression. It was used to quell the Kurdish movement with utmost brutality, to wage wars against Iran and Kuwait, and to put down the Shi'ite and Kurdish uprisings after the First Gulf War.

To sustain such a brutal war machine, successive governments spent enormous amounts of the country's wealth on arms imports from the former Soviet Union during the 1960s and 1970s and later from Western European countries. Despite the fact that military expenditure data in Iraq have always been unreliable, the scant data cited in this chapter indicate that the country has given utmost priority to its military and to military operations. The highest military expenditure occurred in the 1980s, during which an estimated $191.1bn was spent, amounting to an average 46.7 per cent of the GDP of the country. This amount declined to $53.286bn during the 1990s, amounting to 17.8 per cent of GDP. These figures obviously do not take account of the costs of the so-called Popular Army, which reached about 500,000 in the early 1980s (Al-Marashi and Salama 2008) and also the Kurdish auxiliary forces, which reached more than 100,000 men in the late 1980s. The war machine that the

Iraqi government built up also entailed opportunity costs, which were the goods and services that would have otherwise been produced by the men involved in the army. The best and perhaps the most active workforce in society, at some points reaching about 2 million men, was engaged in futile and most of the time destructive war activities. None of the wars that Iraq launched led to any positive political or economic outcomes for the country. To the contrary, they led to widespread destruction of the country's infrastructure and reduced the country's productive capacity to the late 1950s and early 1960s level. The economy shrunk during the entire 1980s and an even worse decline was experienced during the sanctions period of the 1990s and early 2000s. UN sanctions prevented the country from exporting its oil independently, thereby depriving the country of the vital source of revenue that has so far sustained its economy and military.

The likely political and economic outcome of the current war and the consequent political instability that has engulfed the country is not yet certain. The demise of a powerful central government that had managed to suppress various incompatible and to a certain extent uncompromising ethnic and religious components of the country has lifted the lid on a pressure pot. In a similar manner to the former Yugoslavian experience during the 1990s, a dictatorial central government is no longer acceptable to the varied components of Iraqi society. Therefore, in the absence of a clear political framework that guarantees the democratic rights of each component, the need for establishing a new and powerful army would become an overriding priority of the new regime. In an ironically similar experience to Britain's in the early 1920s, the US has been calling for the creation of a new 'Iraqi military *adequate* [emphasis added] for national defense, but [one that] would not countenance a huge, unrepresentative force that suppresses Iraqi's citizens and threatens her neighbours' (Bremer 2006). However, the history of the politics and the military of the country shows that its military has never been a true representative of its incompatible components. Therefore, the prospect of creating a professional army that would possibly not be used to suppress its citizens and threaten its neighbours is far-fetched. Iraq, if the US manages to keep the lid on its troublesome components by force, will remain an unholy marriage of adversaries waiting to erupt in new conflicts in the near future. Its future army, as its best organised institution, will not remain idle should that eruption take place.

6

Syria: The Costs of the Palestinian Question

The military and the state

Similarly to many other artificially created states of the Middle East, present-day Syria was carved out of the Ottoman Empire by France and Britain at the end of the First World War. Syria has always been on the route of trade between the West and East. Nonetheless, until the end of the Second World War, there had never been an independent Syrian state. In the past, the area currently known as Syria was part of the Egyptian, Assyrian, Persian, Roman, Arab, Mameluke, Ottoman and French empires. The word *Syria*, which was the Greek and Roman name for the province in that area, was widely known by the Arabs as *Sham* (Hopwood 1988).

The French's carving out of current Syria was not based on a particular national identity. Syria is indeed a patchwork of various ethnic groups with diverse traditions and religions. The largest group in the country is that of Arab Sunni Muslims who thought along the line of the Ottomans in their fear of non-Muslim minorities. The Shi'ite minority, the Alawite, live in the vicinity of Latakia from which the politically dominant Al-Asad family comes from. They form about 12 per cent of the country's population. The other important minority are the Druze who live in the Jebal Druze area of the south. The Druze are an offshoot of Isma'lism, a Muslim sect widely viewed as heretical by Sunni Muslims. The northeastern part of the country is dominated a conglomeration of various minorities, including Kurds, Armenians, Assyrians, Greek Orthodox and certain Arab tribes. Among the minorities, the Kurds pose a distinctive problem to the state because of their linguistic and ethnic differences from the majority Arabs. Kurds in Syria are predominantly Sunni Muslims, but some adhere to other religious beliefs such as Christian,

Yazidi and Alawite. They have strong cultural and linguistic ties with other Kurds in Turkey, Iraq and Iran rather than with Arabs.

The country became nominally independent in 1941. Despite an election held in July 1943, the country was not completely free from France. The French control of the *Troupes Spéciales du Levant* limited sovereignty in national defence until 1946 when France withdrew its forces from the country.

The origin of the Syrian army goes back to these *Troupes Spéciales*, an internal security force used by France to keep order during the mandate period. The *Troupes Spéciales* were a small 5,000-man Syrian army led by men who were either trained in Ottoman or, later, in French military academies. This small force largely consisted of volunteers from Syrian minorities such as the Kurds, Armenians, Circassians and others. The force was under French control until the end of the mandate.

After independence, the army was expanded to include volunteers as well as conscripts. Until Asad's coup in 1970, the leadership of the army came from the the upper echelons of Syrian society. Names such as Azm, Attasi, Kuzbari and Nizam Al-din that appeared as representatives of influential families in the parliament also populated the top echelons of the army. However, the sectoral representation of the army did not balance political power in the wider society because, unlike in neighbouring countries, the army was never looked upon as a springboard to political office. While the army in Iraq sprinted into the political sphere of the country during the 1930s, the Syrian army was not regarded as a political force by the civilian authorities until it took power in a coup in 1949. Indeed, when the top brass of the army initially issued a note of protest to President Shukri al-Quwatli in 1949, Quwatli remarked that army officers were acting like 'village *mukhtars*' in petitioning the government.

The first clash between the civilian government and the military began after the Arab defeat in the war with Israel which is widely called the '*Nakba*' – meaning disaster or catastrophe in Arabic. In Syria, the army was blamed for the defeat and apparently the head of the Socialist Co-operative Party in the parliament had attacked the army's performance in the war. The army on their part blamed politicians for the lack of resources, poor logistical organisation and the lack of coordination with other Arab armies. The top brass of the army regarded blaming the army for the defeat as an attack on its military honour and issued a note of protest to President Quwatli. When the government ignored the army's protest, senior officers of the army, led by Husni al-Zaima, seized power on 29 March 1949 and established the first military dictatorship in the country.

Zaim's rule lasted just four and a half months. During this short period, he tried to expand and strengthen the army. He also had ambitious towards elevating himself to the rank of historical figures such as Napoleon Bonaparte and Mustafa Kemal of Turkey. His eccentric style and extravagance alienated his supporters. Torrey (1964) argues that Zaim was earnestly trying to form a government under the leadership of a civilian political leader, but politicians were unwilling to do more than express support for the new order. In his short reign, Zaim adopted many social, legal and tax laws that made the traditional ruling class apprehensive. These included land reform, the abolition of hereditary *waqf*, and the introduction of income taxes on personal income and industrial and commercial profits. Zaim also ordered cuts in the swollen governmental bureaucracy, reduction of the number of deputies in the parliament, extending suffrage to educated women, more scrutiny into criticisms of government officials' behaviour, and aspired to adopt a modified Ataturk-style secular system in the country. His ambition was to strengthen the army and equip it with modern armaments. The army was therefore expanded from 5,000 before the coup to 27,000 men afterwards and Zaim proposed a correspondingly higher budget for the army.

In his brief rule, Zaim appeared to have antagonised the traditional ruling class of landowners, urban notables and religious groups alike. His rule was not based on or aligned with a particular political party and attracted little organised social support. Lacking the political skills required for such a position and coming from the Kurdish minority, his policies and proposals, though radical by 1940s standards, were not received well. His rule was brought to an end on 14 August 1949 by another military coup which was led by colonel Hinnawi. Zaim was summarily executed along with his Prime Minister, Muhsin al-Barazi.

Hinnawi's hold on power was short and he immediately handed back the government to civilian rule and promised that the army would never again interfere with the business of the government. A new civilian government was formed under the premiership of former president Hashim al-Atasi and an election was held on 15 November in which the Populists won the majority of seats in the parliament. Hinnawi's influence on the new civilian government and the army didn't last long and he was deposed on 19 December 1949 by Colonel Adib Shishakli, a collaborator of Zaim who fell out with him just a few days before his execution. Ostensibly, Shishakli was unhappy with the new government's move towards some form of Arab unity with Iraq and Jordan. The general fear of a Hashimite takeover of Syria emanated from the Royalist claim that since Faysal was crowned king of National Syria at the end of the First

World War, his grandson Faysal II was the legal king of Syria. Shishakli claimed that the coup was necessary to safeguard the security of the country because Hinnawi and some political leaders were conspiring against the country with foreign elements. Unlike Hinnawi, Shishakli didn't promise that the army would go back to its barracks completely but declared that the army had no intention of interfering in politics unless necessary.

Shishakli was an exponent of a republican non-sectarian state and stood against the Hashimites' expansionist aspirations. During his four-year rule, he undermined the power and the prestige of the traditional ruling class and gradually moved the country towards the left. He continued some of the social reform policies of his former friend and collaborator Zaim, including policies on income and inheritance tax and attempts to provide credit facilities for farmers in financial difficulties. State-held land was ordered to be sold or rented to farmers at a low cost. He also introduced industrialisation policies that encouraged economic growth.

Shishakli's rule was ended, after prolonged political instability in the country, on 26 February 1954 by army officers led by Colonels Abu Asaf and Faysal al-Atasi. The usual political game proceeded by dissolving Shishakli's Arab National Movement party and the old 1950 parliament was reconvened on 15 March; army officers dismissed by Shishakli were reinstated. This led to the rise of the army's dissatisfaction with civilians' heavy-handed interference in its affairs.

The free election which was held on 24 September brought a civilian government back into power. The new parliament comprised a mixed bag of traditionalists and pan-Arab political parties; none had a majority of seats. In fact, independent candidates won 64 out of the overall 135 seats. Perhaps influenced by the emerging Ba'ath Party, the new political forces were in favour of closer ties with Egypt, which led to a defence pact between the two countries on 2 March 1955. The pact was essentially a response to Iraq's joining the Central Treaty Organisation (widely known as CENTO) with Turkey and Pakistan. The nationalisation of the Suez Canal and the tripartite invasion of Egypt by France, Britain and Israel raised the position of Egypt amongst the Arabs, while President Nasser's prestige as the Arab hero who stood up to the imperialist powers reached a peak. Though Syria didn't participate in the war, the war brought the two countries ever closer.

The union between the two countries which was proclaimed on 1 February 1958 put both the army and civilian rule in Syria in a precarious position. The union was tantamount to Nasser's – and an Egyptian – takeover of most political decision-making in both countries. The

'Egyptianisation' of the army and the loss of its autonomy threatened its prestigious status and if continued would have removed it from the political stage in Syria. Army officers, mainly those with traditional and conservative leanings, resented Nasser's complete power over their destiny. Therefore, it didn't take long for the project to go wrong as various political groups and army officers who were marginalised by Nasser started to conspire against it. To make matters worse Nasser relied on the tough Syrian intelligence chief Abd al-Hamid Sarraj as his strongman. The army's discontent started to grow and on 28 September 1961 it marched on Damascus and brought the union between the two countries to its fatal conclusion.

The so-called *infisal* (separatist) regime restored to power the traditional politicians, who captured the parliament and the government. Hinnebusch (2001) argues that the new regime in Damascus represented an effort to turn back the political clock a decade. Banks and industries were de-nationalised and large tracts of land expropriated under the land reform were returned to big landlords and in some places peasants were driven out of their villages. The other competing political groups, though, may have not been completely happy with the union, and resented the separatist regime. The strongest amongst them, the Ba'ath party, suffered most from the adverse effects of the union with Egypt. Its intellectual, urban-based leadership represented by Michel Aflaq, who accepted Nasser's demand to dissolve the party, lost the confidence of many party activists. The party was gradually reduced to its original rural core which was strongly represented by regional branches and army officers who came from those regions. A strong influence amongst them was the party's branch from Alawite-dominated Latakia. Though the Ba'ath party was not ready to take power through a mass revolution, it relied on its 'military committee' to take power on 8 March 1963. One event that inspired it was the Ba'ath party's coming to power through a military coup in Iraq on 8 February 1963.

The weakness of the new regime quickly exposed it to political infighting and competition between different factions; this culminated in another military coup in February 1966, led by Salah Jedid. The new coup sealed the fate of the party's moderates, represented by Aflaq and Salh ad-din al-Bitar. The new coup moved the country away from middle-class and liberal-minded urban-based politicians towards regional peasant-based politicians and army officers. This transformation from the pan-Arab ideologically motivated founders of the party towards a regional and rather sectarian faction paved the way for the dominance of the Alawite sect in both the party and the government. The dismal performance of the army in the 1967 war with Israel and the loss of the Golan Heights further polarised the sectarian Alawite-dominated regime. Within the sect, Hafiz al-Asad eventually consolidated his own power by launching a decisive military coup against the radicals in the party in November 1970 and appointed himself the first Alawite president of the country.

In his 30-year rule, Hafiz al-Asad managed to do what other political and military rulers failed to do. As with Saddam Hussein's rule in Iraq, Asad concentrated the political, executive and military power in the hands of his close followers and relied heavily on the Alawite sect from Latakia. The army was purged of officers who may have posed a threat to his rule and the old party's radical pan-Arab core was swept away. Aflaq and al-Bitar were sacked from the party and were lucky to slip out into exile. Asad eventually built up the so called '*jama'a*' or clique of Alawite personal followers, often his kin, appointed to crucial military and security commands. Similarly to Saddam Hussein's actions, this policy served a dual military and political purpose. On the one hand, the military ability to launch another coup was severely curtailed and on the other hand the party's intellectual squabbles and divisions were brought to an end by completely eliminating the intellectual environment conducive to dissent. The sole political, executive and military power in the country was the president. He became the general secretary of the Ba'ath party and as the president he had the power to dismiss any government or army officers he wished to. The Alawite 'barons' around him were gradually transformed into a presidential clique with clientele relationships with the Alawite minority. Asad therefore successfully subordinated the army to his rule and distanced it from the day-to-day affairs of political life.

Asad, however, was aware of the fact that the Golan Heights, which were lost to Israel in 1967, would not be gained back with a weak army and without the help of other Arab countries, particularly Egypt. To build his army, he required a source of financial help, for which he approached the Gulf countries and Saudi Arabia in particular. Internally, he established the so-called National Progressive Front to include communists, Nasserites and Arab socialists. Asad also built a strong relationship with the Soviet bloc and with the help of the oil-rich Gulf countries' aid he built up the military's capabilities. By the mid-1980s the army possessed 5,000 tanks, 650 combat aeroplanes, 102 missile batteries and had over half a million men under arms (Hinnebusch 2001). Again, like the Ba'ath party's rule in Iraq, Asad successfully pacified the army but maintained it to be used as an instrument of power and suppression. With the exception of few short periods in the 1940s and 1950s, the army has never been distant from political power. It has either been in power, or has maintained the power of a dictator.

The perceived security threats to the country

Overall, Syria participated in the three Arab wars against Israel in which the Syrian army was defeated and the outcome was the loss of the Golan Heights to Israel. In its incursion into Jordan in 1970 to support the Palestinians against King Hussein, the army was pushed back by the smaller Jordanian army with the help of the Israelis. In Lebanon, the involvement of the Syrian army has had and still has enormous adverse consequences for Syrian international relations. Perhaps the only military victory that the army had in the past was the brutal suppression of the Islamic opposition in the 1980s, in which tens of thousands were killed and the Islamic opposition to Asad's rule was subdued.

Syria, however, has been involved in other border conflicts with its neighbours since its creation. On its northern border, France ceded Iskanderuna (Alexandretta) to Turkey in 1939. This strained the relationship with Turkey. The relationship has also been aggravated further by the dispute over Syrian rights to a share of the Euphrates' water, which Turkey uses as a political lever over Syria. In retaliation and to apply political pressure, Asad supported the Kurdish guerrilla movement in Turkey and harboured Kurdish Workers Party (PKK) fighters during the 1980s and early 1990s. Under the threat of war from Turkey, Syria was forced to end its support for the PKK in 1998. Since then, the relationship between the two countries has become more amicable. The sources of conflict, however, are far from being resolved to the Syrians' satisfaction.

Syria also participated in the Lebanese civil war which erupted between various sectarian groups in the 1970s. Its support for Palestinian refugee fighters and the Shi'ite militias in the south of Lebanon brought Israel into the conflict. Syria deliberately used the Palestinians and the Shi'ites to provoke and put pressure on Israel. In recent history, its support for Hizbolla during the 2006 Israeli war in Lebanon and its overt and covert interference in Lebanese internal politics has made Syria a pariah state.

Syria has also been involved in conflicts with its Arab neighbours in Iraq and Jordan. As mentioned earlier, in the 1970s Syria invaded Jordanian territories in support of the Palestinian fighters who were attacked by King Hussein. Though the Jordanian army was not a match for the Syrian army, the Syrians withdrew from Jordan under the threat of war from Israel. The problem with Iraq has been less contentious. In the 1950s, the nationalist rulers of Syria were hostile to the Hashemite monarchy in Iraq because of the latter's friendly relationship with the West. However, the rift between the two countries continued even when the Ba'ath party came to power in both countries during the 1960s. The hostility between the two countries, however, was not based on border disputes but rather on ideological differences.

Perhaps the most important and serious threat to Syria has come from Israel. Indeed, the first defeat of the Arabs in the 1948 war with Israel brought the Syrian military to power in 1949 when the civilian government in Damascus blamed the army for its dismal defeat at the hands of a much smaller nation. The loss of the Golan Heights to Israel in the 1967 war and the failure to regain it in the 1973 war has become a central issue for the Syrian government. Syria failed to resolve the issue through political negotiations initiated by the US in the late 1990s during the Clinton administration. Currently, a new round of negotiations, sponsored by Turkey, has begun. The stake, however, is much greater than that in previous negotiations. In addition to the Golan Heights, the Syrian support for Hizbolla in Lebanon and Hamas and Islamic Jihad in Gaza has become a further obstacle. Syria is currently going through a political dilemma in its foreign relations. On the one hand, the Syrian rulers are convinced that the conflict with Israel cannot be resolved through military means and on the other hand, its hard stance in the Arab conflict with Israel, particularly against Sadat's peace agreement with Israel in the late 1970s, makes a peace deal with Israel very hard to sell to its own public.

The state of the economy

The Ba'ath party's economic strategy was built on a Soviet-style model with some concessions to the private sector in the traditional agricultural sector and in trade. Since Asad's rise to power at the beginning of the 1970s, the party's leaning towards the rural sector was ideologically and psychologically motivated. Coming from a minority sect concentrated in a narrow northwestern region of the country, Asad was a village man rather than an urban intellectual. Therefore, similarly to Saddam Hussein in Iraq, he eradicated the intellectual vanguard of the party who represented the urban pan-Arab intellectuals and the party subsequently became sectarian-based and dependent on a narrow geographical region for political power. The early ideologues of the first Ba'ath coup in 1963, Michel Aflaq and Salh ad-din al-Bitar, adopted a strong semi-Soviet-style role for the public sector. The party's slogan, 'Unity, freedom, socialism', meant that the public sector dominated major industries, construction, energy, foreign trade and infrastructure. The private sector was confined to the peripheral role of supporting the state sector. Therefore, major industries in the country were owned by the public sector.

The Syrian economy is still largely state-led. Both public and private sectors are led by the state's direct and indirect rules and regulation that are designed to serve the ruling party's overall objectives. Hinnebusch (2001) argues that the central vulnerability of Ba'athist political economy was that neither public sector accumulation nor taxation produced sufficient resources to finance the state's many commitments. The financial market was also unable to mobilise domestic savings. Therefore, the gap between saving and investment had to be filled by aid from the Gulf countries and the former Soviet Union.

Table 6.1 shows that the economy enjoyed a respectable growth rate during the 1970s. Indeed, the growth rate of the economy during this period was higher than the growth rate in the rest of the Middle East. Several factors contributed to this remarkable economic prosperity. Firstly, although Syrian oil exports are small by Middle Eastern standards, the sudden rise of the price of oil during early 1970s led to a substantial rise in the country's oil revenues. Secondly, the oil-rich Gulf States donated large amounts of funds to the so called 'frontier countries' through which Syria benefitted hugely. Thirdly, the import-substitution policy strategy adopted by the government initially produced positive outcomes. High economic growth, however, was not sustainable, largely because it was dependent on external sources of finance and the fluctuations of primary commodity markets.

During the 1980s, oil prices crashed and the country's oil revenues declined. This also affected the abilities of the Arab donor countries to continue their financial commitments to other Arab countries. Another factor which reduced the country's income was the Iran-Iraq war and the Syrian support for Iran. The oil pipeline transit from Iraq which passed through the country was subsequently stopped and Syria lost an important source of revenue. The combination of these adverse factors and the limitation of the early stage of the import-substitution strategy brought the economy to a standstill. The downturn of the economy was particularly severe when oil prices crashed during 1986–9. As a result, the exchange rate of the Syrian pound plummeted and the inflation rate soared to between 50 and 100 per cent at the end of the 1980s.

The 1990s brought better economic prospects for the country. Syria participated in the first Gulf War to liberate Kuwait from Iraqi occupation in 1991. Though the economy gained little from new regional conditions, the participation in the war had a considerable positive effect

Table 6.1 Average GDP growth in Syria and other regions, selected years, 1970–2005 (%)

Country/region	1970–9	1980–9	1990–9	2000–5
Syria	8.8	2.8	5.7	4.0
MENA	5.97	2.21	4.30	4.50
Latin America	5.71	1.80	2.90	3.70
Sub-Saharan Africa	4.07	2.18	2.04	4.32
South Asia	3.60	5.70	5.38	7.36
OECD	3.71	2.95	2.48	2.32

Source: Calculated from World Bank, *World Development Indicators* (April 2008).

on the country's foreign relations. A window of opportunity suddenly opened for a better relationship with the US and Western European countries. Contrary to the position of Iraq, Syria turned its misfortune after the collapse of its patron, the Soviet Union, to its own advantage and collaborated with the West against Iraq. However, it seems that the collaboration with the US has been most effective politically, rather than being translated into economic opportunities for the country. Economically, Syria received between $4bn and $5bn in aid at the beginning of the 1990s (Kanovsky 2000) which provided a strong stimulus to the economy. Politically, the Syrian intervention in Lebanon against the Iraqi-backed General Aoun's forces was tolerated by the US and Israel, and Syria subsequently played the Lebanon card in its conflict with Israel. It is also important to mention that the government adopted a new investment law in 1991 which provided a more liberalised environment for private investment. The new law permitted repatriation of profits and movements of capital outside government channels. As a result, the economy grew at a higher rate than in other Middle Eastern countries.

By the mid-1990s, the economy slowed down largely in response to the continuation of old bureaucratic obstructions, corruption and punitive currency laws. As Figure 6.1 shows, in 1999 the economy shrank by about 3.6 per cent compared with average 4 per cent economic growth in the rest of the region. By the beginning of the new millennium, Syria's political and economic problems reverted back to the 1960s era. The country's alignment with Iran and its covert interventions in Iraq after the latter's occupation by the US and its allies isolated the country further. The effect of these new conditions for the economy was that the country largely remained out of the globalisation loop. Similarly to most other

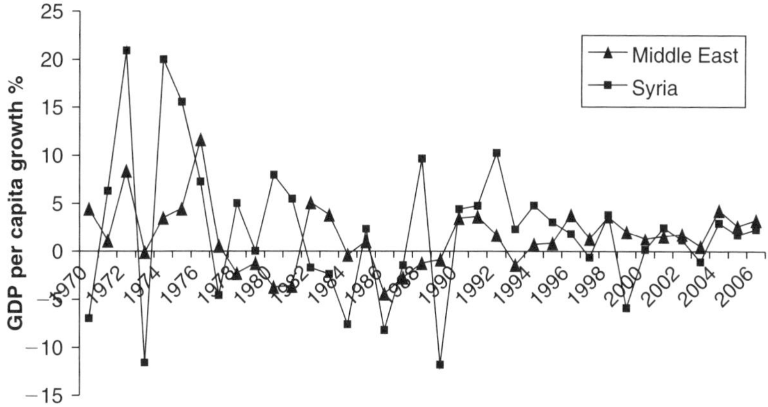

Figure 6.1 GDP per capita growth in Syria and the MENA region, 1970–2006
Source: Calculated from World Bank, *World Development Indicators* (April 2008).

countries in the region, political instability and the lack of will to come to some kind of peace agreement with Israel have deprived the country of foreign sources of investment.

The country's relative isolation from the rest of the world and its economic stagnation, combined with high population growth, severely affected the standard of living of its citizens. Figure 6.1 shows that economic instability throughout the period 1970–2006 resulted in large fluctuations in GDP per capita income. As Hinnebusch (2003) argues, these combined economic and political factors have created an economic dead-end. Indeed, the average nominal GDP per capita growth during 1996–2006 has been just about 0.8 per cent, which is far lower than the sub-Saharan African average GDP per capita growth of about 1.5 per cent during the same period. Considering the population growth rate of 2.7 per cent during the same period, this amounts to an annual deterioration of the standard of living of about 2 per cent.

Military expenditure

Modern Syria has been profoundly affected and shaped by its simmering conflict with Israel. While Jordan and Egypt, after three failed wars, have signed peace treaties with Israel and have subsequently settled their territorial disputes, the Syrian conflict with Israel is far from being resolved. Although the analysis of the causes of diplomatic failure between the two countries is beyond the scope of this book, it is important to note that as other Arab countries and the majority of Palestinians are coming to terms and explicitly or implicitly recognising the state of Israel, Syria now stands alone in this conflict. The failure of the pan-Arab project and a lack of a unified strategy on how to deal with Israel have isolated Syria. Perhaps the biggest blow to the Syrian position was the Egyptians' unilateral peace agreement with Israel in 1979. The Syrian hope of a joint operation with Egypt against Israel was completely dashed. Therefore, regaining the Golan Heights from Israel became the sole responsibility of the Syrian government. In other words, the Golan Heights became a Syrian-Israeli rather than an Arab-Israeli problem.

Syria considered Egypt's unilateral agreement with Israel as a blatant betrayal of the Arab cause. In response, Syria approached other governments in the region, but with no significant impact on the conflict. In 1978, in attempt to outmanoeuvre Egypt, Syria approached its ideological rival, Iraq. In 1979, the two countries announced their intention of creating a union between themselves and of setting up committees to study the project. However, it didn't take long for the old animosity to surface and in a few months Saddam Hussein suspected Asad of being involved in the August coup attempt against him; the relationship between the two countries was severed. As the war broke out between Iraq and Iran, Syria sided with non-Arab Iran; that created an even bigger rift between Syria and majority Arab public opinion. Militarily, Asad was convinced that his country had to rely on its army as a deterrent and as a show of force against any surprise attack by Israel. Therefore, despite all the economic and internal political problems that his country suffered from, disproportionate resources were allocated to defence and the army.

Despite the economic difficulties of the country, military expenditure rose steeply after the first oil-price rise in 1973, which peaked in 1980. The expenditure, however, declined during the 1980s until the mid-1990s, when it started to rise again. A word of caution must be expressed here; as in the cases of other countries discussed in this book, the data should be regarded only as an indicator of trends in military expenditure. As Cordesman (2006) argues, Syria used to get concessional arms sales and loans from the former Soviet Union and the Warsaw Pact countries; therefore, the full costs of its armaments and defence expenditure are almost impossible to verify.

Military expenditure during the 1970s

Hafiz al-Asad came to power in the late 1970s. As a military man, his aim was to strengthen the army, recover the Golan Heights from Israel,

Table 6.2 Syrian defence expenditure, 1970–89, in $m, at 1978 prices and exchange rates

Year	Military expenditure	Percentage increase	GDP growth rate (%)	ME as a percentage of GDP
1970	429	–	–3.8	9.6
1971	370	–4.0	9.9	8.4
1972	427	15.4	25.0	8.2
1973	661	54.8	8.6	14.9
1974	624	–5.6	24.1	13.8
1975	1,116	78.9	19.5	16.2
1976	1,110	0.0	11.0	15.2
1977	1,111	0.0	1.3	15.3
1978	1,165	4.9	8.7	14.5
1979	2,018	73.2	3.6	21.1
1970–9	9,031			

Sources: World Bank, *World Development Indicators* (April 2008); SIPRI, *Yearbook* (1980, 1981).

and consolidate his grip on power. He followed these aims with great tenacity. Until then Syria was poor in resources and was largely agrarian. Building a strong army equipped with modern armaments to match those of the Israelis in the early 1970s was beyond the financial means of his country. The 1973 war with Israel, in which Syria failed to regain the Golan Heights, marked a turning point in the military's fortune. One the one hand, the Arab joint action in the oil market quadrupled the price of oil and Syria's oil exports, though modest by other Arab oil-exporting countries' standards (500,000 to 600,000 barrels a day), became the main source of foreign exchange for the country. On the other hand, as mentioned earlier, the oil-rich Gulf countries started supporting the so-called 'the frontier' countries adjacent to Israel, and Syria benefited hugely from their financial backing. This subsequently led to unprecedented increase in military expenditure of the country. According to the Stockholm International Peace Research Institute (SIPRI), in 1973 Syrian military expenditure jumped from 8.2 per cent of GDP of the country in 1972 to about 15 per cent. In real terms this amounted to an increase to $661 million from $427 million. In terms of manpower, Asad increased army numbers to 170,000 men on the eve of the 1973 war. The dramatic increase in expenditure by about 79 per cent of GDP in 1975 was indicative of the lag of expenditure which was fuelled by the earlier influx of aid from the Gulf countries and the Soviet Union. However, the influx of aid was not necessarily translated into investment and economic growth. The sudden economic growth experienced in the mid-1970s dissipated as quickly as it came. In the late 1970s, economic growth in the country declined sharply and indeed the economy shrank by 1.27 per cent during 1977. Despite this economic downturn, spending on defence continued to increase until it peaked at $2.018bn in 1979. In total, military expenditure during the 1970s amounted to $9.03bn. This figure obviously does not take into account the costs of the military hardware destroyed during the 1973 war, the infrastructure damages sustained by the country's oil installations, and the opportunity costs of engaging more than 300,000 men in the war machine.

Military expenditure during the 1980s

As discussed earlier, during the 1980s Syria suffered a double economic and military blow. On the one hand, Egypt under Sadat signed a peace agreement with Israel and thereby effectively ended the possibility of Egypt getting engaged in another war with Israel. Syria therefore lost a very strong ally with which it had co-ordinated its past wars against Israel. On the other hand, the war broke out between Iraq and Iran and Syria aligned itself with the non-Arab Iran, an arch enemy of the US and Israel. Syria subsequently lost the sympathy of the oil-rich Gulf States who came under serious threat from the new, zealous Shi'ite-Islamic government in Tehran. Aid from the Gulf States was subsequently reduced. This coincided with the crash of oil prices in the international oil market. Syria, therefore, no longer had the financial luxury it had in the 1970s to acquire new weaponry for its expanding army.

Syria, however, was not engaged in direct military confrontations with Israel in the 1980s but continued a proxy war in Lebanon. The Syrian army's entry into Lebanon in 1976 was a precursor of the Israeli invasion of Lebanon in 1982. Syria supported the Palestinian Liberation Organisation (PLO) and the Lebanese Shi'ite armed groups against the Maronite groups. The threat from Lebanon prompted Israel to respond to a call from the then Maronite President Bashir Gemayel and mounted a full invasion of Lebanon ion 6 June 1982. Syria, although avoiding full military confrontation with Israel, was nevertheless engaged in sporadic fighting with the invading army. Before further escalation in the confrontation, Syria quickly agreed to the ceasefire with Israel on 11 June despite repeated pleas from the PLO and Lebanese groups. This showed that Syria was not prepared to risk a direct full-blown war with

Israel at the time when its traditional Arab allies, Egypt and Jordan, were distancing themselves from the prospect. Syria, therefore, was truly left on its own and was politically and strategically isolated from other Arab countries.

The effect of this continued hostility on military expenditure was grave. As Table 6.3 shows, Syria continued its high military spending, inherited from the 1970s. Its objective was to achieve some form of military parity with Israel as a deterrent rather than as an aggressive military gesture. Syria subsequently acquired new surface-to-surface missiles from the Soviet Union and almost doubled its army in size from about 300,000 men in 1983 to about 500,000 in 1985.

The 1980s also witnessed the rise of Islamic fundamentalism in the country. In a reprisal for an assassination attempt on Asad's life in 1982, security police killed scores of Islamic prisoners, which led to an all-out confrontation between the army and Muslim activists in the city of Hama. The army later unleashed its wrath on the city and subdued it by using helicopter gunships and tanks in operations in which an estimated 20,000 civilians and 1,000 solders were killed. The harsh suppression measures used by the government attracted international condemnation. Politically, however, the suppression of domestic dissent, particularly ideological dissent, consolidated Asad's powers further at a time of an economic downturn. Table 6.3 shows the extent

Table 6.3 The Syrian defence expenditure, 1980–9, in constant $m, 1988 prices and exchange rates

Year	**Military expenditure**	**Percentage increase**	**GDP growth rate (%)**	**ME as a percentage of GDP**
1980	3,960	20.0	12.0	17.3
1981	3,635	–8.2	9.5	14.7
1982	3,526	–3.0	2.1	15.6
1983	3,511	0.0	1.4	15.4
1984	3,582	2.0	–4.1	16.7
1985	3,152	–7.4	6.1	17.2
1986	2,573	–20.0	–5.0	17.7
1987	1,601	–8.0	1.9	11.2
1988	1,482	–10.0	13.3	7.9
1989	2,070	2.4	–9.0	8.0
1980–9	29,090			

Sources: World Bank, *World Development Indicators* (April 2008); SIPRI, *Yearbook* (various years); SIPRI, *Military Expenditure Database.*

of the economic instability during 1980s. With the exception of a few short, intermittent periods, the 1980s witnessed an unprecedented contraction in the economy. By 1989, the economy had shrunk by 9 per cent and the country had accumulated $15bn in military debt to the former Soviet Union.

Despite economic hardship, the government continued to spend huge amounts of the country's scarce resources on the army. Although military expenditure started to decline from 1985, spending still stood at about 8 per cent of GDP. In total, the country spent $29.09bn during the 1980s, which amounts to 3.2 times its spending during the 1970s.

Military expenditure 1990–2006

The first Gulf War in 1991 brought some relief to Syria. The country unexpectedly agreed to participate in the US-led allied forces that ended the Iraqi occupation of Kuwait. Subsequently, Syria was rewarded with large payments from Saudi Arabia and other Gulf States. According to the Washington Institute for Near East Policy, this aid amounted to $4bn to $5bn (PeaceWatch 2000). This provided some economic stimulus during the first half of the 1990s. The Gulf War coincided with the collapse of the Soviet bloc, the traditional source of arms and aid to the country. As the main source of arms imports was lost, military expenditure was expected by many observers to decline. Nonetheless, Syria's military expenditure increased by an average 4.06 per cent during the decade.

In terms of armament, Cordesman (2006) argues that much of Syria's conventional weapons have become obsolescent or obsolete. In parallel fashion to Iran's experience during the 1990s, Syria resorted to North Korea for Scud surface-to-surface missiles and nuclear and biological weapons technology. The rise of military expenditure is perhaps explained by the country's secret endeavour to build a deterrent arsenal of such non-conventional weaponry. Asad therefore failed to reinvent himself and use the reconciliation of 1991 with the West to the country's full benefit. The strengthening ties with Iran and North Korea isolated the country further and pushed the country's peace negotiations with Israel to an impasse. Military expenditure continued to rise despite the collapse of the Soviet Union. In 1990, it increased by 46.9 per cent. Though it declined during 1992 and 1993, it stabilised at about $4bn at the end of the decade. By the beginning of the millennium, military expenditure continued to rise despite a lack of sources of conventional arms imports. Table 6.4 shows that the country on average spent $3.468bn annually during the 1990s and $6.112bn annually during 2000–6. The rise of the threat of Islamic terrorism at the beginning of the millennium and the US-led invasion of Iraq in 2003 brought Syria to worldwide attention. The US administration declared Syria to be part of the 'axis of evil', along with North Korea and Iran. The US subsequently imposed various trade and banking sanctions against the country.

The Syrian economy currently faces high rates of inflation, a lack of vital foreign investment and a gradual decline in the technology and skills required for ambitious economic growth. Militarily, Syria's competition with Israel remains pointless and, as Cordesman (2006) argues, Syria has created 'hollow' armed forces with obsolete weaponry that could only be effective in low-level skirmishes in Lebanon or against internal civilian opposition to the state. The military expenditure represented by its percentage of the GDP of the country has declined considerably compared with its level during the 1980s though it is still above 5 per cent of GDP.

Table 6.4 Syrian defence expenditure, 1990–2006, in constant $m, 2005 prices and exchange rates

Year	Military expenditure	Percentage increase	GDP growth rate (%)	ME as a percentage of GDP
1990	3,040	46.9	7.6	6.0
1991	4,907	61.4	7.9	9.1
1992	4,544	–7.4	13.5	7.9
1993	3,603	–20.7	5.2	6.4
1994	3,884	7.8	7.7	6.5
1995	3,916	0.8	5.8	6.2
1996	3,638	–7.1	4.4	5.2
1997	3,750	3.1	1.8	5.0
1998	4,062	8.3	6.3	5.1
1999	4,124	1.5	–3.6	4.8
1990–9	39,468			
2000	5,418	31.4	2.7	5.5
2001	5,018	–7.4	5.2	4.9
2002	5,056	0.7	4.0	4.7
2003	5,887	16.4	1.6	5.5
2004	7,137	21.2	5.8	6.0
2005	7,011	–1.8	4.5	5.3
2006	7,328	4.5	5.1	5.1
1990–2006	42,855			

Sources: World Bank, *World Development Indicators* (April 2008); SIPRI, *Yearbook* (1988); SIPRI, *Military Expenditure Database*.

Conclusion

For 30 years, Asad senior ruled Syria through the military and other security apparatuses. Though not unique, his rule shaped the country's current internal and foreign political trajectories. The Alawite monopoly of power led to the alienation of the rest of the nation and one-party rule effectively created a dictatorial regime. Such a regime is still exclusively dependent on the army and other government security organisations.

Though Asad managed to distance the army from political power, the army remained the instrument of power and coercion in both internal and external political spheres. To secure the loyalty of the army, Asad initially purged its top echelon and elevated officers from an Alawite background to commanding positions. According to Zisser (2001), at the time of his death in 2000, more than 90 per cent of the army generals were from an Alawite background. Therefore, the army no longer posed a direct threat to the government.

Asad's peace of mind, however, was achieved at enormous cost to his country. The failure to resolve the conflict with Israel through peaceful means put Syria in a precarious position. With a weak regional and international position, he resorted to strengthening the army at any cost. He subsequently allocated enormous amounts of the country's scarce resources to the military. The analysis in this chapter shows that the country annually spent an average $4.843bn in real terms in the period 1990–2006. Indeed, the country's average military spending during the 2000–06 period was even higher than its average spending during the periods of direct confrontation with Israel. The relentless drive for building a stronger military power has put a great deal of pressure on the country's economic development and the standard of living of its citizens. World Bank statistics show that at the end of 2006, GNP per capita income of $1,560 was exactly at its 1980s level.

Hafiz Asad's legacy remains to haunt the country for the foreseeable future; he effectively created a presidential monarchy through elevating his son, Bashar al-Asad, to power. The country's huge army uses up a disproportionate amount of the country's resources. As mentioned earlier, perhaps the only success that the army has achieved in its long and very expensive history could be its victory over the civilian rebellion in the city of Hama in the early 1980s.

The Syrian government continues to pursue the same failed policies of the past. It ostensibly tries to acquire biological and nuclear weapons through collaboration with Iran and North Korea, two countries that have been blacklisted by the US. The country's deteriorating international reputation has further been exacerbated by its intervention in Iraq after the US-led invasion of the country in 2003. The country still has no winnable military and political position in the region and there is little indication that the military and the ruling Alawite sect are willing to relinquish their grip on power.

7
Egypt: The Costs of Being an Arab Leader

The military and the state

Until the beginning of the First World War, Egypt was an autonomous region of the Ottoman Empire ruled by hereditary rulers called Khedives. Though Britain had occupied the country since 1882, it was at the beginning of the First World War that it ended Ottoman authority over Egypt and declared it a protectorate. The political framework for Egypt was provided by the constitution of 1923 which declared Egypt a hereditary monarchy. Britain retained substantial control over the country's foreign policy, the Suez Canal, and its defence against foreign aggression. The 1936 Anglo-Egyptian Treaty moved the country to independence. The Treaty however, ensured that the two countries formed a military alliance and that Egypt would co-operate with Britain on foreign affairs. Under the terms of the Treaty, Britain was to retain a garrison in the Canal Zone for 20 years.

One of the results of the 1936 Treaty was the opening of the Egyptian Military Academy to secondary-school graduates who passed a competitive examination regardless of their class background. This opened the way for students who were from modest backgrounds and with nationalist sympathies to join the academy. Amongst them future leaders such Gamal Abd al-Nasser and Anwar al-Sadat rose to prominence. A secret association, the 'Free Officers' society, was established amongst army officers that graduated from the academy, and had a profound influence on the future of the country. The exact date of the establishment of the society is uncertain but some believe that it was established after the defeat of the Arabs in the first Palestinian war in 1948 (Goldschmidt 1988).

By the end of the Second World War, the new Egyptian army, though it had grown in number to more than 22,000, was ill-equipped and not prepared for any serious combat. In 1948, the army was pushed into the war in Palestine without any strategy or co-ordination with other Arab armies and was badly defeated by the highly organised Israeli army. By the beginning of the 1950s, the internal political conditions of the country were quite unstable and to a large extend unsustainable. The monarchy's corrupt regime led to the alienation of the vast majority of Egyptians. That situation, coupled with the humiliating defeat at the hands of a smaller country, increased political instability and street violence to unprecedented level. Yapp (1996) argues that by 1952, the army was called upon to take the place of police and deal with street violence, defending a government and a system in which the Free Officers had no confidence. Although the Free Officers lacked a clear ideology they were bound by a set of clear and unequivocal objectives. Amongst them the elimination of the presence of Britain and of its supporters in Egypt was an overriding objective. Internally, the aim of the Free Officers was to eliminate feudalism and establish healthy democratic life in the country. The Free Officers, however, were not clear about the type and the nature of the democratic government they aspired to bring about. Unlike their Iraqi and Syrian contemporaries, the new military officers who plotted for political change behind the scenes in Egypt were very young and inexperienced. Therefore, to make themselves more acceptable to the wider public, they resorted to a much older army officer, General Muhammad Najib, as a nominal leader and representative. By 1950, the Free Officers elected Najib as President of the Officers Club, against the wishes of the King. The King had become concerned at the rising prestige of the officers, and rejected a later a proposal to make Najib Minister of Defence. On 23 July 1952, the army launched a military coup and removed the monarchy from power. The Free Officers, however, did not overthrow the monarchy in alliance with any particular political party. Vatikiotis (1961) argues that the army's coup was so decisive and confident that the monarchy's supporters didn't have the time and the means to obstruct it.

The 23 July coup was neither a popular revolution nor was it backed by a popular political party. Goldschmidt (1988) argues that the military coup was indeed the result of what was happening in the army rather than of events in the rest of the country. However, this didn't mean that the Free Officers were not influenced by the wider social and political problems in the country. The traditional *wafd* government was demoralised and incompetent and the country was headed by a corrupt monarch. Land ownership was concentrated in the hands of the royal family and minority landowners who mostly lived outside Egypt. The majority of the peasantry ('*Fellahin*') lived in poverty. The country had also acceded part of its sovereignty to Britain through a long-term treaty which was not accepted as being fair by the wider public.

In the political sphere, the Islamic Brotherhood, which was established at the end of the 1920s, was making huge political gains at the expense of secular political parties. The communists, though not influential as such, were promoted by the rising influence and reputation of the Soviet Union and the rise of other communist parties in the Middle East. In a similar way to other Middle Eastern countries, as Vatikiotis (1961) argues, the army was the only well-organised institution that could provide law and order and was the only dynamic force in a disrupted society.

As mentioned earlier, the Free Officers were largely young and inexperienced. In 1952, the most prominent member of the association, Gamal Abd al-Nasser, was just 34 years old; he lacked experience of how to run not only a country but the army itself. Therefore, when the coup occurred, the Free Officers handed the Egyptian government over to an old regime but issued a call to political parties to improve their performance, purge themselves of undesirable elements and declare publicly their reconstituted structure and political platform. Within a year the monarchy was completely abolished and a military dictatorship was established. Despite this, the consolidation of power in the hands of Nasser was not an easy process. Nasser first had to cleanse the military junta of undesirable elements that may have posed a threat to his authority. By April 1954, when Nasser became the Prime Minister, Nagib's authority had weakened; however, he was kept as the president of the republic to placate public sentiment. The influential Muslim Brotherhood was also dissolved by a decree after an assassination attempt on Nasser in October 1954. At the same time, Nagib was removed from power and placed under house arrest. By the end of 1954, all political opposition had been suppressed and the military junta was exclusively ruled by Nasser. This sealed the fate of the country; it was in the hands of a military dictatorship represented by Nasser himself.

By the beginning of 1956, the junta adopted a constitution which formulated their main ideas and aspirations as to how to govern the country in the future. The constitution, adopted by plebiscite on 23 June 1956, included a call for the abolition of imperialism and feudalism, an end to capitalist control over the government and the establishment of a strong army. In foreign relations, the new rulers of the country alarmed Britain and France, while the US adopted a friendly approach to Nasser. Goldschmidt (1988) argues that after the anti-Mossadeq coup in Iran, the US actually facilitated Nasser's takeover. The Suez crisis of 1956, during which Egypt attempted to reclaim its ownership of the Canal Zone, led to a tripartite invasion of the country by Israel, France and Britain. The invasion rallied the Egyptian public around Nasser. The US's support of Nasser proved to be vital, though it did not necessarily come at the behest of Egypt itself. The US immediately demanded an Israeli withdrawal and an end to the invasion. The Suez crisis therefore raised Nasser's domestic credentials despite the military defeat and the destruction of most of the army's newly acquired aircraft. The Suez conflict also raised Nasser's prestige in the Arab world, particularly among the Palestinians, who were looking for an Arab leader bold enough to stand up against imperialism and Zionism.

By the end of the 1950s, Nasser had managed to establish his cult-figure status in Egypt as well as in other Arab countries. As a result, other Arab military dictators inspired by his prestige tried to establish their own cult-figure versions in their own countries – Abdul Karim Qassim in Iraq, Hafiz al-Asad in Syria and Mo'ammar al Qathafi in Libya followed Nasser's lead.

Nasser died on 28 September 1970 before the country's political impasse with Israel could be resolved. Egypt was not prepared to negotiate directly with Israel and did not abandon its support for the Palestinians. However, the army's rule continued after his death when his close comrade Anwar al-Sadat was chosen as his successor. Sadat was one of the few Free Officers to have survived Nasser's political upheaval. His rule started with a purge of military officers who were in opposition to his policies, and his immediate concern was the Arab-Israeli conflict. The October war of 1973 with Israel marked the beginning of a new chapter in Egypt's foreign policy and its position as leader of the Arab countries. Yapp (1996) argues that Sadat was able to claim that he had achieved victory, restored the army's prestige and vindicated Arab honour by crossing the Suez Canal. After the war, Sadat was convinced that a military settlement of the hostilities with Israel was impossible. Therefore, he adopted radical steps to deal with Egypt's foreign and internal policies. Economically, acknowledging the failure of public-sector economics, he adopted the so-called '*infitah*', directing policy towards trade and investment. As a result the economic growth rate accelerated to an average seven per cent per annum from 1973 to 1980. Politically, Sadat encouraged political and press freedom and raised the possibility of a multi-party political system. During his time in power, Egypt's foreign policy and relations were also changed. With the help of the US, Egypt was engaged in negotiations with Israel, secured a partial Israeli withdrawal from Sinai and recovered vitally needed oilfields. In a dramatic gesture, Sadat visited Jerusalem in November 1977 and addressed the

Israeli parliament, the Knesset. The move angered Palestinians and Arab countries alike. He subsequently paved the way for a departure from the hitherto close pro-Soviet relationship towards closer ties with the US and Western European countries. His change of foreign policy culminated in the Camp David agreements of September 1978 and 1979 in which a peace treaty was signed with Israel which ensured the complete evacuation of Israel from Egyptian territories. Sadat was assassinated by an Islamic organisation on 6 October 1981 and was succeeded by his close associate and his vice-president Hosni Mubarak. Mubarak was also an army officer though not a member of the Free Officer association. He pledged to continue the *infitah* policy of his predecessor and restored some kind of electoral representation in 1984. The army, though not as strongly represented in the government as it had been during Nasser's period in office, has remained loyal to Mubarak.

Perceived security threats to the country

Egypt no longer faces any external threat from its neighbours. Signing the 1979 Camp David Treaty with Israel effectively ended the hostilities between the two countries. The Treaty also implicitly ended the de facto leadership status of Egypt amongst the Arab countries; the reputation that Nasser established for the country as the leader of the Arab countries and Egypt's assumption of responsibility for the Palestinian problem in effect was ended by the recovery of the Sinai Peninsula. The economic and political rewards for the harmonisation of the relationship with Israel were far-reaching. Since then, the US has directed billions of dollars in military and economic aid to Egypt and the country no longer faces any economic or trade restrictions from Western countries. Politically, however, the undemocratic regime continued to govern and human-rights violations in the country appear to have been condoned by the US and its allies.

The only real threat to the government is domestic rather than external. The country is currently facing the threat of Islamic terrorism from the Gama'a al-Islamya (the Islamic Group or IG) which has targeted the lucrative tourist industry. The country has also faced increasing hostility between the ethnic Coptic minority and Islamic activists which has sporadically erupted in violence.

Given the low level of internal threat and the absence of any tangible external threat to the country, the legitimate question is: does the country really require a very strong, large and expensive army any more?

The state of the economy

During the late 1950s, in response to various international political and economic obstacles, the government moved away from relying on the private sector as the main engine of growth, and state intervention and influence became increasingly important (Ikram 2006). However, it took the Free Officers about a decade to fully gear the economy towards virtually complete state control. This major move occurred in 1961 when the state nationalised the banking sector and 44 companies in basic industries and acquired large stakes in other companies engaged in commerce and light manufacturing. The move was called the 'Socialist Revolution' by the Free Officers.

The objectives of the so-called socialist revolution adopted by the Nasser regime were to achieve an annual GDP growth rate of 7 per cent, an equitable distribution of wealth, and a speedy development of education, health and other social services. The central-planning strategy didn't achieve its intended aims due to a combination of internal and external factors. However, it is important to mention here that in addition to the inherent limitations of central planning itself, the strategy failed to produce the desired outcome due to, among others things, as El-Ghonemy (2003) argues, the failure of cotton production, the main agricultural commodity of the country, the diversion of investment from the commodity-producing sector to armament purchases for the 1962–7 war in Yemen and the 1967 war with Israel, the withdrawal of the US aid and dwindling revenues from tourism. Therefore, the average rate of growth of the economy declined to 3.6 per cent by 1970 from 6 per cent during the 1962–7 period.

Economic conditions had deteriorated by the beginning of the 1970s. The budget deficit was rising and was increasingly financed through borrowing from the banking system, rising inflation was eroding real wages and standards of living, and the country's external debt was on the rise despite the flow of aid from the Arab oil-exporting countries. As a result, as Figure 7.1 shows, between 1972 and 1974, the economy grew at an average rate of 1.74 per cent, 1 per cent lower than the rate of population growth. This prompted Sadat to adopt the *infitah* policy mentioned earlier. The aim of the policy was to offer the private sector a much wider role in the economy and encourage foreign investment, particularly financial capital from Arab oil-exporting countries. Subsequently, the government adopted a relatively relaxed approach to foreign trade, foreign investment and private enterprise. Ikram (2006) states that the policy was not in fact meant to engineer a fundamental shift in government economic policy. The aims of the policy were rather modest. It was principally designed to attract surplus Arab funds into the economy.

The result was spectacular economic growth which peaked at 14.6 per cent in 1976. By the end of the 1970s, economic growth continued at an average 6 per cent per annum at a time when the rest of the MENA-region economies were on a downturn. However, Ikram argues that the economic recovery owed little to the *infitah* strategy because the state's grip on the economy remained as strong as ever. Indeed, privatisation of the publicly owned industries was not on the agenda at the time and it seemed that the government was not completely sure about the direction of the economy when the *infitah* policy was adopted. The adoption of the strategy, however, coincided with the recovery of the oilfields in the Sinai Peninsula and the rise in the price of oil. This provided the government with large windfalls of foreign exchange earnings and gave a strong impetus to the economy in general. At the same time the demand for skilled and semi-skilled workers from the oil-exporting countries increased substantially, and this led to a significant rise in workers' remittances. The Arab oil-exporting countries (which included Saudi Arabia, Kuwait, UAE and Qatar) also provided substantial amounts of aid to the country through the Gulf Organisation for the Development of Egypt.

During the 1980s, economic growth remained high relative to other MENA countries. Table 7.1 shows that while economic growth in the rest

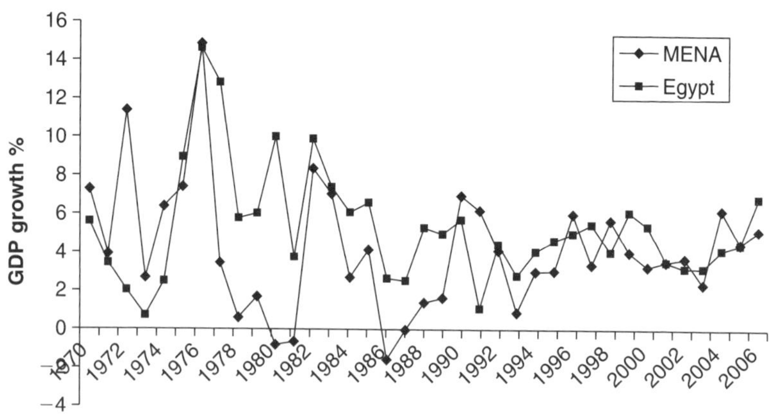

Figure 7.1 GDP growth in Egypt and MENA region, 1970–2006
Source: Calculated from World Bank, *World Development Indicators* (April 2008).

Table 7.1 Average GDP growth in Egypt and other regions, selected years, 1970–2006

	1970–9	1980–9	1990–9	2000–6
Egypt	6.2	5.9	4.3	4.4
MENA	6.0	2.2	4.3	4.5
Latin America	5.7	1.8	2.9	3.7
Sub-Saharan Africa	4.1	2.2	2.0	4.3
South Asia	3.6	5.7	5.4	7.4
OECD	3.7	3.0	2.5	2.3

Source: Calculated from World Bank, *World Development Indicators* (April 2008).

of MENA averaged 2.2 per cent per annum during the decade, the average annual economic growth rate in Egypt was 5.9 per cent. A stable environment for economic growth was maintained by a large amount of aid from the US, external borrowing, the relatively high workers' remittances, particularly from Iraq, and the expansion of the tourist sector.

The end of the 1980s marked the beginning of economic and financial difficulties for the country. The decline of international oil prices led to a substantial decline in the country's foreign exchange earnings. Non-oil exports did not increase sufficiently to compensate for the loss of oil revenues. The government increasingly relied on foreign borrowing to stimulate economic growth. By 1988, the country's long-term debt amounted to $39.08bn with an annual debt service of $2.11bn. Similar to the experience of many other developing countries, Egypt at the beginning of the 1980s serviced its debt by new borrowing and almost half of its new foreign borrowing was paid towards its debt service obligations. As foreign creditors gradually lost confidence in the ability of the economy to repay and the country's debt arrears accumulated, foreign lending dried up. By the end of the 1980s, economic growth was slowing down and the country sought debt forgiveness and debt rescheduling to deal with the mounting debt crisis.

By the beginning of the 1990s, debt and the unsustainable government budget deficit began taking their toll on the economy. The economic problems of the country were aggravated further by the outbreak of the Gulf crisis in 1990 and the decline in the country's workers' remittances. As a result economic growth declined to 1.08 per cent in 1991. The effects of slow economic growth and high population rates on the standard of living were grave; real income per head declined by 20 per cent from $750 in 1986 to $640 in 1989 and to $600 in 1990.

In 1991, Egypt concluded a standby agreement with the IMF and a structural adjustment programme with the World Bank, officially called the Economic Reform and Structural Adjustment Programme (ERSAP). The main aims of the programme were to reduce the country's external debt and budget deficit to manageable levels. In essence, the conditionality of the agreed programme required the government to abandon the state-led economic strategy inherited from Nasser and adopt a market economy. This required cutting state subsidies, privatisation of state-held industries and liberalisation of trade and financial markets. The government subsequently reduced its budget deficit from 15.3 per cent of GDP at market prices in 1991 to 0.9 per cent in 1997. Ikram (2006) argues that the sharp decline was brought about by a reduction in public expenditure and an increase in government revenues. The biggest proportion of the reduction of public expenditure was borne by government investment. Government subsidies for essential foodstuffs such as bread, wheat flour, sugar and cooking oil were also cut. Though a full account of the economic changes during the 1990s are beyond the scope of this book, it is important to note that GDP per capita income growth during the decade averaged 2.4 per cent. With population growth hovering around 2 per cent, real per capita income hardly changed during 1990s.

By the beginning of the millennium the economy's growth rate slowed down to an average 3.2 per cent, though better economic growth was experienced from 2004 to 2006. The economic decline of the early 2000s can largely be attributed to the structural weakness of the economy and the heavy reliance on foreign sources of income. For instance, as El-Ghonemy (2003) argues, the government had no control over the foreign demand for Egyptian labour and the erratic nature of workers' remittances, the country's oil revenues were subject to international price fluctuations, and the country's tourist revenues were adversely affect by the sporadic Islamic terrorist killings of tourists and the effects of the September 11, 2001 attacks. This slowdown in the economy was temporarily reversed by a rise in the price of oil and an increase in the country's external borrowing. According to the Central Bank of Egypt, in 2005 the country's total oil revenues increased to \$10.222bn from \$5.229bn in 2004, while non-oil export revenues declined by \$301 million at the same time that the country's total foreign debt increased to \$29.592bn from \$25.083bn.

At the end of 2006, the economy's performance had hardly moved from its historical pattern. The economy remained dependent on foreign sources of income, the inflow of foreign loans and workers' remittances raised the rate of inflation and eroded gains achieved in the standard

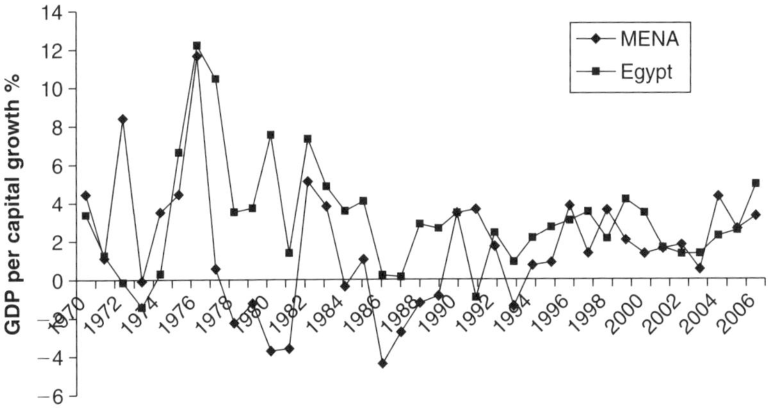

Figure 7.2 GDP per capita growth in Egypt and the MENA region, 1970–2006
Source: Calculated from World Bank, *World Development Indicators* (April 2008).

of living, while the absence of a viable alternative to commodity dependence led to erratic economic growth rates. In terms of per capita income, economic growth has barely been translated into an improvement in the standard of living. In 2006, gross national income per capita was lower than its year 2000 level by about 7 per cent, and that was about half of the MENA average per capita income.

Military expenditure

Between independence and 1970, Egypt went through three major wars; the 1948 war when Israel declared statehood, the 1956 Suez Crisis in which France, Britain and Israel invaded the country and the 1967 war with Israel. Egypt was militarily defeated in the three wars as the Egyptian army was not a match for the Israeli, British and French armies and did not have the quality of foreign support that Israel enjoyed. Though defeated, the outcome of the 1956 war for Egypt was morally different from the other two wars. In 1956, Egypt was defending its territorial integrity and was invaded by three superior armies. As mentioned earlier, under US pressure, the war was ended and Egypt claimed a notional victory which consolidated Nasser's grip on power. The outcome of the other two wars left scars on the Egyptian military's pride. Egypt was defeated badly and lost the Sinai Peninsula and its most important and badly needed oil fields to Israel. The effects of these wars on the country's military expenditure and the role of the army was far-reaching.

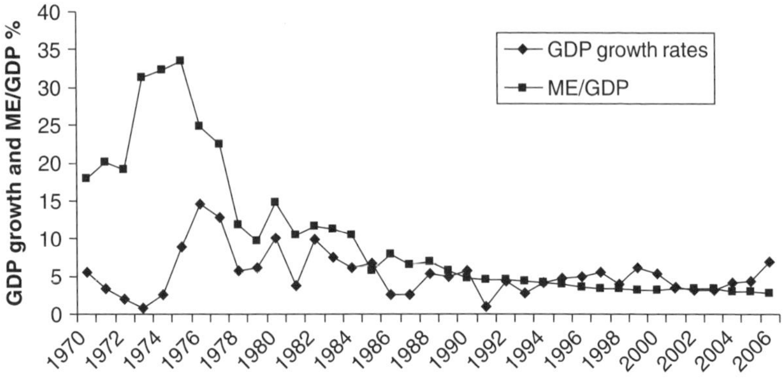

Figure 7.3 GDP growth rate and military expenditure as a percentage of GDP in Egypt, 1970–2006

Sources: SIPRI for military expenditure as a percentage of GDP; World Bank, *World Development Indicators* (April 2008) for GDP growth rates.

Military expenditure during the 1970s

Until his death, Nasser's resolve to defeat Israel and liberate Palestine didn't show any sign of waning. At his death, the country boasted a large army, an unresolved military conflict and a drive for acquiring more sophisticated and expensive armament that was stronger than ever. According to SIPRI, during the 1970s the country on average spent 23.6 per cent of its GDP annually on the military. The date shows that highest expenditure ratio was incurred during and after the October War. During 1973 when GDP growth was at its lowest ebb, the country spent 31.4 per cent of its GDP on the military. At 1978 prices and exchange rates, this amounted to $5.367bn annually. The high expenditure continued until the beginning of the peace negotiations with Israel which culminated in the signing of the Camp David Treaty in 1979. Subsequently, military expenditure as a percentage of GDP, in real terms, was 36.6 per cent lower than its previous level. Though boycotted and shunned by most Arab countries, Egypt prudently turned its back on the pan-Arab project which was thought by Nasser's successor, Sadat, as a non-viable goal. The shrinking of the military burden, as Figure 7.2 shows, led to a peace dividend as more resources became available for other public expenditures. However, the social result of the peace dividend was not that straightforward as peace itself does not guarantee better allocation of resources. Cohen and Ward (1995) argue that the resource dividend seems not to have diffused very widely through the Egyptian political economy. Indeed, as the figure shows, economic growth rates during 1978 and 1979 were half of the economic growth rate of 1977. The question is, therefore: Where did the money go? Although Cohen and Ward argue that the answer lies in the high population growth rate in the country, this seems implausible as the cut in military expenditure was dramatic while the population growth rate was consistent over the decade. However, one must bear in mind that Egypt at the end of 1977 was going through turmoil in its relationship with the IMF. The food subsidy cuts of the 1977 recommended by the IMF led to widespread street violence – known as 'bread riots' – which slowed down the economy, and the country had to resort to foreign sources of funds for investment. Therefore, between 1977 and 1980, the country's foreign outstanding debt more than doubled, from \$7.51bn in 1977 to \$14.693bn in 1980, and the country's debt-service burden increased from \$454.1 million in 1977 to \$1,069 million in 1980. At the end of the decade, it seems that increasing foreign debt and debt service, combined with long periods of excessively high military expenditure and the rigid structure of the economy, all took their toll on the economy. The combination of all these factors limited the peace dividend that the country was expected to enjoy after the massive defence cuts.

Table 7.2 Egyptian defence expenditure, 1970–9, in \$m, at 1978 prices and exchange rates

Year	**Military expenditure**	**Percentage increase**	**GDP growth rate (%)**	**ME as percentage of GDP**
1970	2,271	–	5.6	18.0
1971	2,972	31.0	3.4	20.1
1972	2,911	–2.1	2.0	19.2
1973	5,367	84.4	0.7	31.4
1974	5,927	10.0	2.5	32.4
1975	5,756	–3.0	8.9	33.4
1976	5,004	–13.1	14.6	24.9
1977	5,238	5.0	12.8	22.5
1978	3,322	–36.6	5.8	11.8
1979	2,790	–16.0	6.0	9.6
1970–9	41,558			

Sources: World Bank, *World Development Indicators* (April 2008); SIPRI, *Yearbook* (1980, 1981).

Military expenditure during the 1980s

The military expenditure burden during the 1980s declined considerably in relative terms. On average, the country spent around 9.1 per cent of its GDP on the military in this period, a rate less than half that of the 1970s. In real terms, however, military expenditure was still relatively high. On average the country's military expenditure amounted to an annual $5bn. Military expenditure continued to grow during the decade by an average 5.6 per cent per annum. This rate of increase was matched by an equal growth rate in the economy. Therefore, economic growth allowed the government to deploy an increasing proportion of GDP for the military sector. On the other hand, it is also true that the large standing army of the country required a substantial amount of resources to be maintained even in the absence of an urgent need to acquire new armaments. After the signing of the Camp David Treaty with Israel and contrary to expectations, Egypt did not downsize its army. Indeed, according to Stork and Paul (1983), the government expanded its army during the 1980s by more than 100,000 men and bought an extra 1,000 tanks. Therefore, as the external threat of a war receded during 1980s, the continued high military expenditure was completely unwarranted. One, therefore, could not infer that a guns-butter trade-off would automatically occur. Indeed, a

Table 7.3 Egyptian defence expenditure, 1980–9, in $m, at 1988 prices and exchange rates

Year	Military expenditure	Percentage increase	GDP growth rate (%)	ME as percentage of GDP
1980	4,091*	46.6	10.0	14.7
1981	5,392	31.8	3.8	10.5
1982	5,442	1.0	9.9	11.7
1983	5,889	8.0	7.4	11.2
1984	6,070	3.0	6.1	10.4
1985	5,252	–13.1	6.6	5.8
1986	5,013	–5.0	2.7	7.8
1987	4,607	–8.1	2.5	6.5
1988	4,089	–11.2	5.3	6.9
1989	4,222	3.3	5.0	5.8
1980–9	50,067			

Note: * estimated figure.
Sources: World Bank, *World Development Indicators* (April 2008); SIPRI, *Yearbook* (1990); SIPRI, *Military Expenditure Database*.

structural change from a war to a peace economy requires a fundamental transformation of the political economy of the country and a true change in the economic and political emphasis of the state. In the late 1980s, there was little or no evidence that Egypt had made any groundbreaking fundamental change in its political economy decision-making to enable it to fully benefit from the peace opportunity it achieved in the late 1970s.

Military expenditure 1990–2006

Military expenditure as a percentage of GDP continued to decline during the 1990s. On average the country spent 3.95 per cent annually of its GDP on the military. This rate obviously excludes the military assistance that the US offered the country each year. In real terms, the country on average spent about $2.238bn on the military annually. The data show a visible decline of military expenditure during the decade relative to the 1980s. As mentioned earlier, due to regional factors and economic mismanagement, economic growth was relatively lower during the 1990s. Indeed, given the rate of population growth rate of 1.91 per cent during the decade, the real rate of economic growth was barely above 2 per cent. The 1990s' economic difficulties were manifested by high external and internal deficits. As mentioned earlier, Egypt suffered a double blow in its external revenues; one the one hand, the decline of the price of oil in 1986 to about $12 a barrel from about $36 a barrel at the beginning of the 1980s slashed the country's oil revenues, and on the other hand, the reduction in workers' remittances, particularly after the Iran-Iraq war, reduced the country's ability to service its external debt. In response, Egypt resorted to external borrowing to service its existing debt. At the end of the 1990s, the country had accumulated a relatively high foreign debt. According to the World Bank, the country's foreign debt amounted to over $37bn at the end of the 1980s and the annual debt service obligation of the country was estimated to be about $2.6bn. The OECD put the foreign debt figure at $50bn. In response, Egypt adopted the World Bank's Economic Reform and Structural Adjustment Programme. With the help of the IMF, the World Bank and other donors, the country aimed at stabilising the economy by reducing the inflation rate, reducing budget and external deficits and ultimately achieving higher economic growth. The point here is that although the distinction between military and civilian debt is very difficult if not impossible to make, the level of military expenditure pursued at a time of economic

Table 7.4 Egyptian defence expenditure, 1990–2006, in $m, at 2005 prices and exchange rates

Year	Military expenditure	Percentage increase	GDP growth rate (%)	ME as percentage of GDP
1990	2,360	–	5.7	4.7
1991	2,249	–5.0	1.1	4.6
1992	2,376	5.6	4.4	4.5
1993	2,328	–2.0	2.8	4.3
1994	2,310	–1.0	4.1	4.2
1995	2,172	–6.0	4.6	3.9
1996	2,044	–5.9	5.0	3.5
1997	2,073	1.4	5.5	3.3
1998	2,215	6.8	4.0	3.3
1999	2,250	1.6	6.1	3.2
1990–9	22,377			
2000	2,405	6.9	5.4	3.2
2001	2,571	6.9	3.5	3.3
2002	2,689	4.6	3.2	3.4
2003	2,816	4.7	3.2	3.3
2004	2,665	–5.4	4.1	3.0
2005	2,659	0.0	4.4	2.9
2006	2,674	0.0	6.8	2.7
1990–2006	40,856			

Sources: World Bank, *World Development Indicators* (April 2008); SIPRI, *Military Expenditure Database.*

crisis was hardly justified at a time of little or no external threat to the country.

The country however, did not scale down its military despite the economic difficulties suffered. On the contrary, World Bank data shows that the country started enlarging its army from the mid-1990s. Figures show that the army's personnel was increased to 610,000 in 1995 from 450,000 in 1989. The number was increased further to 680,000 by the end of the decade. It is also worth mentioning that the unemployment rate started rising at the end of the 1980s. By the mid-1990s, it was estimated to be 11.3 per cent compared to 6.9 per cent in 1989. The expansion of the army's manpower in the mid-1990s seems to have been a deliberate policy to absorb this rising unemployment and by the end of the decade, unemployment had reduced to 8.1 per cent, a reduction of 3.2 per cent from the 1995 level. A fact that supports this conclusion is that the economic growth rate in the second half of the decade was on average lower than its rate in the first half. Therefore, the source of the reduction in the unemployment rate was surely not high economic growth rates.

Military expenditure at the beginning of the millennium started to increase and on average the country spent $2.640bn on the military annually compared with an average of $2.238bn during the 1990s. This increase, however, may not be a result of higher arms imports. SIPRI data on arms transfer shows that although Egypt was ranked amongst the highest conventional weapons recipients in the world (sixth in the rankings), the value of its conventional arms imports remained at around $600 million a year during 2000–6. The military expenditure burden measured by the ratio of military expenditure to GDP shows a declining trend. Table 7.4 shows that during 2006 this ratio declined to a commendable 2.7 per cent, the lowest level in the country's modern history.

Conclusion

The history of modern Egypt is still inseparable from that of its army. Since the first military coup in 1952, the real political power in the country has rested with the leadership of the army. Since then, the three army officers, Nasser, Sadat and Mubarak, who have ruled the country pursued different political and military goals, at various economic and social costs. Early on, Nasser's anti-British strategy paid off during the Suez Canal war but his pan-Arab strategy completely failed to unify various Arab countries under his leadership. He also effectively prevented civil society and institutions from developing and banned political parties from operating. His dictatorial regime inevitably served the superpower confrontation in the region. During his era, Egypt spent a disproportionate part of its scarce resources on the military and war preparations. The defeat in the 1967 war with Israel led to further escalation of hostilities and the problem of resource misappropriation got worse on his death in 1970. The analysis in this chapter shows that the country allocated vast amounts of its wealth to military and war preparation during the 1970s. After the defeat in the 1973 war, Nasser's successor, Sadat, changed the overall military strategy and effectively abandoned the regime's claim on liberating Palestine and championing the pan-Arab cause. The signing of the Camp David Treaty with Israel in 1979 marked the end of the pan-Arab project in general and the removal of one of the important causes of external threat to the country – and the associated high military expenditure. The peace agreement with Israel, however, isolated Egypt from the rest of the Arab countries, albeit temporarily, but also enhanced the country's international status. Western countries and the US started offering a range of bilateral and multilateral military and economic assistance to the country. Unfortunately, the expected peace dividend did not materialise. The institutional weakness of the centrally planned economy led by the army, coupled with corruption, mismanagement of resources and the absence of transparency and the rule of law, prevented the country from harnessing the economic opportunities opened up at the end of hostilities with Israel. The army continued to prevent a democratic and multi-party system from developing. High population growth and the country's vulnerability to external shocks made the 1980s and the 1990s a very difficult time for the Egyptian people and the country's economy. The per capita income in the country relative to the average MENA level fell by more than 46 per cent by the beginning of the 1980s compared to its level at the beginning of the 1970s. Bearing in mind that the per capita income in the country was 86 per cent of the average MENA region's level at the beginning of the 1970s, the rapid decline in the relative standard of living marked the beginning of a new economic era for the country. As military expenditure increased during the early part of the 1980s, the ratio tumbled to a mere 40 per cent of the average MENA level by the end of the decade. The country's political claim to leadership of the Arab countries was therefore based on hollow economic conditions.

Sadat's successor, Mubarak, has endeavoured to preserve the internal and external status quo, with various degrees of success. His close ties with the US has ensured the continuation of US military and economic assistance to the country but his internal status has been weakened by increasing levels of poverty, ethnic and religious violence, incidents of terrorism, human-rights abuses and lack of democracy. The characteristic common to the three successive military dictators, moreover, has been mistrust of civilian rule. They have effectively prevented democratic and civil institutions from developing and entrusted the destiny of the country to the military.

By the end of 2006, per capita income in the country is still at 60 per cent of the average MENA-region level and, according to the World Bank, about 47 per cent of the population is living on under $2 a day. The army, which has been in power for an uninterrupted 56 years, is presiding with impunity over a period of economic underdevelopment, mismanagement of resources and political misadventures. Up to the end of the 1970s, the state of war with Israel empowered the army politically and ostensibly justified its grip on power. Following the end of hostilities in 1979 the fact that it has remained in power, or behind political power, has become a fundamental hindrance to the economic and social development of the country. Sporadic eruptions of violence, riots by the poor and political discontent have become a permanent means of expressing civilians' alienation from political power; their frequency may increase if fundamental political changes are not adopted in the near future.

8
Israel: The Costs of Survival in a Hostile Neighbourhood

The military and the state

The state of Israel was established and sustained by the use of force and the power of its army. Effective and continuous foreign power assistance has been an essential ingredient of that process. Formally known as the Israeli Defence Forces (IDF), the Israeli army has been instrumental in the making of the state of Israel. Even before the proclamation of the state on 14 May 1948, most Jewish leaders in the Zionist movement had the conviction that military power and the use of force were key factors in their statehood. Indeed, as history shows, the use of force and military superiority was the midwife of the new Jewish state and is still Israel's only guardian.

The origin of the IDF goes back to the 1920s when Jewish immigrants in Israel, known as Yishuv, established a defence force to defend Jewish settlements against Arab attacks. The defence force was called the Haganah ('defences' in Hebrew). Since the British mandate forbade the Jews from bearing arms, the Haganah remained a clandestine organisation. The defence organisation was originally formed by the Histadrut (the Jewish Federation of Labour) and came under the control of civilian rule in 1929. Until very late, Yishuv wanted the Haganah to remain a defensive force and refrain from taking any offensive action against the Arabs or British forces occupying Palestine. The Jewish settlements and communities therefore were defended by stationary forces against Arab invaders who frequently raided their settlements and villages. As persecution of the Jews by the Germans in Europe intensified during the 1930s, Jewish immigration to Palestine increased and the population of Jews in Palestine swelled to 400,000 in 1937 compared with just 175,000 in 1932 (Schiff 1987). The defensive nature of the Haganah was not uniformly accepted by all Jews, particularly during the Arab revolt which began in 1936 and when the Jewish settlements and villages sustained more systematic attacks from the Arabs. Subsequently a group of militants broke off and formed a group called Irgun Zvai Leumi (National Military Organisation) or IZL. This group was eventually disbanded when they decided to cooperate with Britain after the outbreak of the the Second World War.

The important turning point in the Haganah's strategic thinking, Tal (2000) argues, occurred in December 1946 when David Ben-Gurion, Head of the Jewish Agency, assumed the defence portfolio. In his address to the 22nd Zionist Congress in December 1946, Ben-Gurion outlined his strategy and called for the creation of a regular military force that would be able to resist the invasion of the regular Arab armies when Britain withdrew from Palestine. He considered such an army as essential for the survival of Israel. Until then, only Palmah, the strikeforce arm of the Haganah, was a regular force and the remainder consisted of irregular and voluntary forces. The shift of the strategy was specified in the Order of National Structure, issued by the Haganah Command in November 1947, stipulating the transformation of the Haganah into a national army. The new army was based on compulsory mobilisation of the Jewish population and charged with confronting regular armed forces. On 26 May 1948, the Israeli Provisional Government issued Order No. 4, which established the Israeli Defence Forces and prohibited the existence of any other armed forces within the country. The order effectively transformed the Haganah into a formidable regular armed force.

The first major war that IDF took part in was the 1948 war of independence against the Arab countries. The Jewish Agency was certain that the regular Arab armies would invade Palestine upon the declaration of the state of Israel; therefore, Ben-Gurion was keen on changing the Haganah into a regular armed force with a compulsory mobilisation mandate. Haganah, however, was a battle-hardened semi-regular force with strict ideological adherence; the Nazi holocaust was an important factor in strengthening the resolve of the Israeli fighting force. The vast majority of Jewish emigrants were Europeans who had personally experienced, or their relatives and acquaintances had, the Nazi anti-Jewish policy. Some Russian Jews also had memories of the pogrom campaigns against them at the beginning of the century. Therefore, the Jews were fighting when they had their backs against the wall whereas the Palestinian Arabs had the other Arab countries to flee to if they were pushed.

The so-called war of independence, which Arabs call the '*Nakba*' ('catastrophe'), lasted until 7 January 1949. It was a long and costly war for the new state in which 6,000 soldiers and civilians, or 1 per cent of the entire Jewish population, lost their lives. Shlaim (2000) contests the conventional Zionist version of the war. He argues that Israeli propaganda and the conventional Zionist version of the war held that the war was an unbalanced war between seven regular armies and a small, infant and unprepared state. The reality was very different from what is still taught in Israeli education. In terms of military balance, it is portrayed that the war was a struggle between too many Arabs and two few Jews. In reality, the total number of Arab regular and irregular forces including Palestinians militia and regular Arab armies totalled 25,000 fighters in mid-May 1948 whereas the IDF consisted of over 35,000 fighters. By mid-July the IDF had mobilised 65,000 fighters and this number was increased to 96,441 soldiers by December of the same year (Shlaim 2000). In terms of war planning and leadership the IDF had a well-organised central command and structure, whereas the Arab armies lacked co-ordination and Arab leaders were motivated by self-interest. The Israeli leadership was aware of the divisions among the Arabs and exploited it whenever possible. When the Arabs were defeated, the Israeli leadership dealt with each Arab country on its own rather than collectively and signed an armistice agreement with each separately.

The 1948 war was won by Israel militarily and politically. Jewish leaders prudently accepted the United Nations Partition Resolution that stipulated the creation of the state of Israel whereas the Palestinian leadership, represented by the Arab Higher Committee (AHC) lead by the Grand Mufti of Jerusalem, Hajj Amin al-Husseini, rejected the Resolution. The rejection effectively ended their chance of having an independent state for a long period. At the end of the war, the West Bank was occupied by Jordan, which was in essence the prime war aim of the King of Jordan, King Abdullah, and the rest of country was occupied by Israel. The war also led to the displacement of large numbers of Palestinians.

Both the military and political triumph in their first major war and Arab weakness bolstered the Israeli leadership's resolve not to just ignore Arab opinion but to embark upon a policy of coercion and aggression in dealing with its Arab neighbours. The Israeli involvement in the Suez Canal War against Egypt was unwarranted and Israel was motivated by territorial greed at the expense of Egypt. Though the military victory in the war had important psychological effect for the IDF, the political repercussions were negative. Nasser, as indicated in Chapter Seven, came out of the war unscathed and with his prestige strengthened among the Arabs. The Suez Canal War also had international ramifications for the state of Israel as well as for the region as a whole. The Soviet Union for the first time threatened to intervene militarily against Israel if Israel did not withdraw from the Sinai Peninsula; this established a precedent for hostile East-West tit-for-tat policy intervention in the Middle East. Israel also secured some guarantees from the US for its security. Shlaim (2000) argues that the Suez Canal War also had grave impacts on internal Israeli and Arab politics. In Israel, it strengthened Ben-Gurion's hawkish politics and managed to defeat the moderates led by Moshe Sharett, who was a proponent of diplomacy and negotiation with the Arab countries. Amongst the Arab countries, the tripartite aggression (Israel, Britain, France) was considered by Arabs as Israel ganging up with imperialists against the Arab Nation. Therefore, the war galvanised Arab public opinion around the pan-Arab tendency in Arab politics, led by Nasser. This tendency made the likelihood of Israeli co-existence with its Arab neighbours ever more remote.

The two wars made the state of Israel increasingly dependent on its military capability rather than on seeking political recognition through peaceful means with its Arab neighbours. As the political negotiations with the Palestinians and the wider Arab world failed and most Arab countries rejected UN policy on Palestine, Israeli leaders realised that deterrence was the military strategy most important to its survival but that it was not enough to guarantee ultimate future security. Therefore, they sought an external guarantee to their security. Shlaim (2000) argues that the early strong military and nuclear relationship with France was not convincing enough to Ben-Gurion as French politics were prone to change. As a result, he turned to the US for an external security guarantee, which was eventually secured by 1957. The international political atmosphere at the time, especially cold war developments, reinforced the relationship ties between Israel and the US on the one hand and the Arab-Soviet relationship on the other.

At all times, Israel was inferior to its Arab neighbours in terms of economic and human resources. Therefore, the country was less able than the Arabs to absorb the heavy casualties produced by attrition warfare. The military strategy adopted, therefore, was to build a qualitatively superior conventional army to those of the Arab countries. In this context, the ultimate deterrent that Israel has endeavoured to build has been nuclear capability and a policy of preventing its Arab neighbours from acquiring it. The moral-political justification for such an endeavour, Aronson (2000) argues, was anchored in the aforementioned asymmetric character of Arab-Israeli conflict.

It is also worth mentioning that although the Arabs were defeated, they have never willingly accepted the existence of the state of Israel. Israel also was blamed for the gradual intensification of Arab hostility towards its existence. Despite the fact the Arabs called their first all-out war with Israel *Nakba*, there is ample historical evidence that the political milieu was more conducive for negotiations and political settlement during the early years of the state of Israel than later.

The conclusion to be drawn is that as peace was difficult to establish, the existence and maintenance of the state of Israel amid hostile neighbours was only sustained by a strong and technically superior army supported by the covert existence of nuclear deterrent capability. Therefore, unlike other countries of the region where the army hijacked political power and used the conflict with Israel as a justification for the prevention of democratic institutions from developing, in Israel the state has had to rely on its army for its existence. The state of Israel therefore is living under the shadow of war with its neighbours and has to be on alert all the time.

The perceived security threats to the country

No other country in the Middle East faces such fundamental threats to its existence as those faced by Israel. While other countries of the region were carved out of the Ottoman Empire by the mandate powers and they encompassed the peoples of the geographical spaces that the countries were built upon, the state of Israel was created out of Palestine by Jewish people who, mainly, emigrated from Europe. The other contrasting difference between Israel and its neighbours is that the foundations of the state of Israel were laid down during the mandate era, whereas other states of the region were created by the mandate arrangement between the victorious allied powers after the First World War. This created a deep sense of malaise in the region. Israel therefore is widely regarded by the people of the region as an alien country built and effectively imposed by the foreign powers that were traditionally regarded as imperialists and oppressors of the region. The association of Israel with imperialist powers, Britain and France during the 1940s and 1950s, and the US after that, increased the chasm with the wider Middle Eastern public. The use of force and the initial aggressive military strategy of Israel did not help in easing that general feeling. Israel therefore has not been willingly accepted or recognised by the people of the region despite its 60 years of existence. Therefore, the fundamental problem that the country still faces is the legitimacy of its existence. Israel so far has not reached a state of peace with its neighbours. It still occupies the Syrian Golan Heights territory, has pushed millions of Palestinians out of their homeland, and no genuine peace agreement has so far been reached with its immediate neighbours.

The initial threat that Israel faced was the threat of all-out war with the Arab countries. Thanks to the effective military and political external support that Israel has received and its own military strategy, the country has so far survived past wars. The demise of the Soviet Union, an ardent supporter of the Arabs, in the late 1990s also eased the conventional military pressure on Israel, while Arab countries, particularly Syria, lost their close ally and military supplier. However, the recent resurgence of Russia and the close ties that have been revived with Syria may cause discomfort to Israel. Despite all these issues, the proliferation of weapons of mass destruction, especially chemical and biological weapons – the poor man's nuclear bomb – has not been beyond the reach of many regional countries hostile to Israel. Reports indicate that Syria, Egypt and Iran now have stockpiles of such deadly weapons. Iraq during Saddam Hussein's era developed and used weapons of mass destruction in its war with Iran and against the Kurds. To make matters worse, there are clandestine efforts on behalf of many countries of the region to acquire nuclear technology. Though Israel has in the past bombed Iraqi and Syrian nuclear facilities, and Libya has officially abandoned its nuclear ambitions, the Iranian drive to acquire nuclear technology is a big cause of concern for Israel. The fundamental flaw of the Israeli nuclear deterrent strategy is that nuclear superiority does not eliminate the threat of a future nuclear confrontation. Indeed, in the absence of a viable and durable peace agreement in the region, Israel will continue to face the danger of other countries developing or acquiring such technology. Israel therefore has to look out for any sign of weapons of mass destruction acquired by any of its neighbours.

The current war with the Palestinian factions in the Gaza Strip and the previous wars in the south of Lebanon show that, despite its conventional military power superiority, Israel is neither invincible nor immune to future unexpected wars with its immediate neighbours. Since it is not possible for the state of Israel to live or die 'by the sword', the military deterrent can only be used as an instrument to achieve peace rather than to humiliate its neighbours. The founding figures of Israel, particularly Ben-Gurion and Golda Meir, had no understanding of the Arabs, no sympathy with Palestinians, and had no faith in the possibility of peaceful coexistence with them. For Israel to live with itself and with its neighbours there must be a shift in such an unrealistic and uncompromising political and psychological approach. After the 1973 war, the political environment in the region has been more conducive to peace than war but Israel has on many occasions jeopardised realistic chances of achieving a long-lasting peace. Though the discussion of the reasons behind the past Israeli policies towards a peace settlement with its neighbours is beyond the scope of this book, it seems that the Israelis' deep-seated sense of besiegement and insecurity within the region is psychological as well as historical. Psychologically, Israel and the Israeli public have a deep sense of mistrust of their neighbours as well as complete self confidence – 'the Arabs are incapable of doing right but the Israelis are incapable of doing wrong'. Unfortunately, the political debate in Israel most of the time has been resolved in favour of the hawkish factions that advocated the use of force to achieve legitimacy and security. This trend was represented by Ben-Gurion, the founding father of the state of Israel and Golda Meir (Prime Minister, 1969–74). The so-called dovish trend was represented by Moshe Sharett early on, Levi Ashkol during the 1960s and Yitzhak Rabin to a certain extent later; these figures advocated negotiations and peaceful settlement but were let down internally by the intransigence of Jewish politicians coming from a background of persecution in Europe and externally by dictatorial Arab leaders who used the Palestinian issue for their own political ends.

The state of the economy

The Israeli economy is relatively small in size and strongly influenced by the state of war, or near war, that has dominated its existence since its establishment in 1948. The country is relatively poor in natural resources and being boycotted by its neighbours it has little or no economic relationship or integration with the region. The forefathers of the country considered it as a refuge for all Jews of the world regardless of their country of origin or needs. Immigration therefore has been the bedrock of its population increase, leading to enormous costs for accommodation and integration. Jews from Europe were relatively highly skilled, with substantial capital endowments that enriched the country in its early stages, whereas those from the surrounding Arab countries were poor and the least educated. The new wave of immigrants from the former Soviet Union bloc, particularly during the late 1980s and 1990s, were relatively highly skilled but quite poor. The cost of the accommodation and integration of the new immigrants was very high and required heavy government intervention in the economy.

The political economy of the country is largely influenced by the historical nature of its establishment. The country is besieged by hostile neighbours, so security has continuously dominated the political-economic thinking of its leaders. Nonetheless, the economy is far from being completely planned like those of the formerly communist East European countries but it is also not a free market economy in the European liberal sense of the term. The political economy of the country, however, has been profoundly influenced by the Zionist ideology, which has many characteristics of the social-democrat ideology of the late 19th and early 20th-century European labour movement. The socialist Zionists wanted a state with a strong orientation towards public-owned enterprises, but the need for a large-scale inflow of foreign capital to deal with the immediate needs of large flows of immigrants compelled them to accept far-reaching compromises in order to encourage private investment (Sanbar 1990). At the same time, conservatives and liberals wanted a state dominated by free enterprise, but they recognised the need for strong government leadership in times of political and economic emergency. In the first three decades of Israel's existence, the government was dominated by the Labour Party. Therefore, the leaders of the state were guided by high social aspirations and a strong sense of social responsibility. This required strong and effective government intervention in the economy. In principle, the Zionist ideology required the state to provide a safe refuge and humane social environment for long-suffering and persecuted world Jewry. This is significantly different from the causes of the formation of neighbouring, mainly Arab, states in the aftermath of the First World War. Israel was created out of the sense of the need for a homeland for Jews escaping persecution in Europe. Therefore they urgently needed a just, humane and free society, whereas the other countries of the region were artificially carved out from the former Ottoman Empire by Great Britain and France with little or no consideration of the people's needs and aspirations.

Thus, by virtue of its creation, the government of Israel became responsible for the economic welfare of the new immigrants to the country – for the provision of shelter, basic economic needs and security. It is also noteworthy that the early European immigrants brought with them a labour-movement culture of organisation and active labour union participation in the country's political and economic decision-making. Therefore, the Trade Union Federation, Histadrut, became a major player in the economy. Plessner (1994) argues that the socialist nature of the state emanated from three important factors. First, there was virtually no free access to capital markets and capital could only be raised through the government. Second, a substantial proportion of the means of production was owned either by the government or by Histadrut. Third, the wage structure reflected the attempt to implement basic socialist welfare standards.

Guided by this ethos and influenced by the challenges of war and of settling new immigrants in the country, the economy required enormous amounts of foreign capital. This came from three different sources: grants and loans from world Jewry, largely from the US; economic and military assistance from the US government; and German reparation and restitution payments. The unilateral transfer from world Jewry and loans from the US government grew slowly to reach approximately $200 million per annum during the 1950s, whereas German reparations started at $40 million in 1950 and reached $199 million in 1961 (Reiser 1989). Therefore, the country was always in a position to spend more than it could raise by its own means.

In the first 25 years of its establishment, the economy took off, with vibrant growth. Until the beginning of the 1970s economic growth averaged about 9.7 per cent annually (Plessner 1994). However, this buoyant economic growth started to slow down from 1973 and then entered a long period of stagnation and recession. The formerly respectable growth rate was brought to a halt largely because of three internal and external reasons. First, the initial high economic growth mainly emanated from the needs of the new infant state's requirements for infrastructure, basic industries producing consumer goods and vital military installations and industries. Large investments, as mentioned earlier, came from foreign sources, with little cost to the economy. This high growth rates, as Plessner (1994) argues, did not necessarily mean that the economy performed efficiently. The structure of the economy, dominated by heavy government control, was not tested by market criteria. The second reason was the Yom Kippur War in 1973 which raised public expenditure and increased inflation rates. Rivlin (1992) argues that the cost of the Yom Kippur War may have constituted over 75 per cent of 1973's GNP. Over 3,000 soldiers were killed and wounded and many thousand reservists were called up for military service, affecting exports. Defence expenditure was subsequently increased by 66 per cent in real terms. The third reason for the slowdown in the economy were the oil price rises in 1972 and 1973 which increased the costs of the country's imports and subsequently raised the rate of inflation. As a result economic growth slowed to 3.3 per cent in 1973 from 7.3 per cent in 1970, leading to a recession in 1977. Table 8.1 shows that the average economic growth rate during the 1970s was 5.8 per cent. The economic suffering of the late 1970s continued into the 1980s with an unprecedentedly low growth rate of 3.7 per cent.

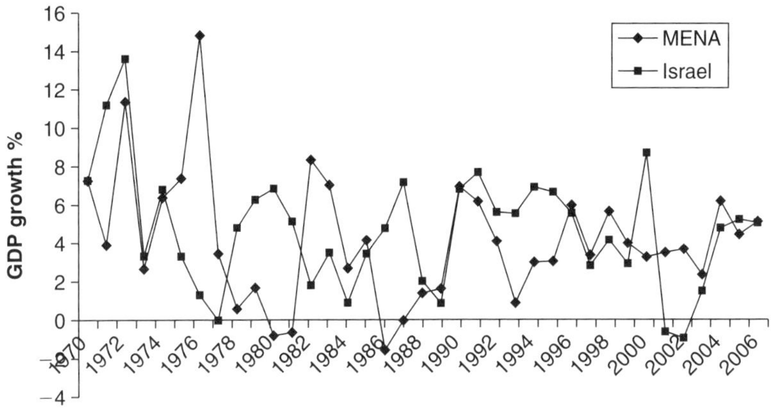

Figure 8.1 GDP growth in Israel and the MENA region, 1970–2006
Source: World Bank, *World Development Indicators* (April 2008).

Table 8.1 Average GDP growth in Israel and other regions, selected years, 1970–2006

	1970–9	1980–9	1990–9	2000–6
Israel	5.8	3.7	5.5	3.4
MENA	6.0	2.2	4.3	4.5
Latin America	5.7	1.8	2.9	3.7
Sub-Saharan Africa	4.1	2.2	2.0	4.3
South Asia	3.6	5.7	5.4	7.4
OECD	3.7	3.0	2.5	2.3

Source: Calculated from World Bank, *World Development Indicators* (April 2008).

In 1977 the Likud coalition came to power, ending nearly 30 years of the Labour Party's social democratic domination. The regime adopted a new approach to the economic problems of the country. Foreign currency controls were abolished, basic commodity and public transportation subsidies were substantially reduced, capital subsidies to export industries were also reduced, the various exchange rates of the currency were unified and an independently floating exchange rate regime was adopted, and the currency was devalued. Though the new policies improved the balance of payments of the country, inflation rates increased, leading to high rates of unemployment and a deterioration in the standard of living. Figure 8.2 shows that by the mid-1980s, the

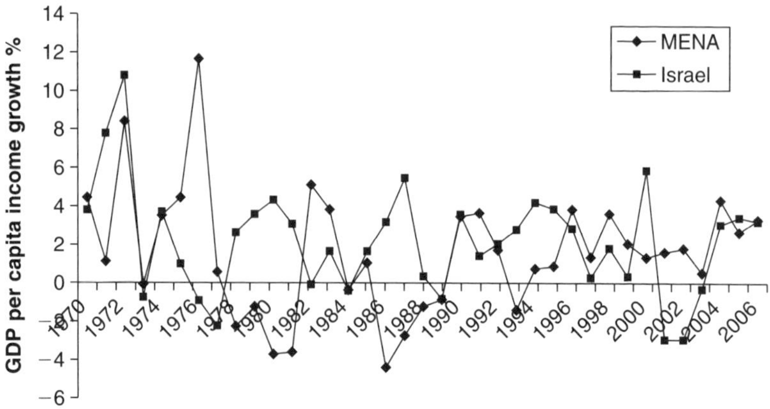

Figure 8.2 GDP per capita growth in Israel and the MENA region, 1970–2006
Source: World Bank, *World Development Indicators* (April 2008).

rate of inflation had rocketed to 373 per cent. High rates of inflation and slow economic growth eroded the standard of living in the country.

To deal with the problems facing the economy a new national unity government was created in 1984. After few short-term measures, the government adopted a comprehensive economic stabilisation programme. The aims of the programme were to deal with the high rates of inflation and the mounting balance of payments deficit and revive the economy. The programme introduced a new national currency, the New Israeli Shekel, sharply cut consumer subsidies, a reduction in real wages and a suspension of the cost-of-living allowance, and strong government budget control (Sanbar 1990). As a result, the rate of inflation was reduced to 48 per cent in 1986 and 20 per cent in 1987, and the balance of payments situation improved. The programme also reduced real wages and private consumption, which subsequently increased the rate of unemployment to a peak of 8 per cent. By the end of the 1980s, the economy had slowed down again and despite a 10 per cent devaluation of the new currency in 1986, real wages started to increase again. By the 1990s, the programme managed to reduce the rate of inflation and stabilise the economy. The early 1990s also witnessed the demise of the former Soviet bloc and the relaxation of restrictions on the immigration of Jews from Russia. As a result 400,000 Jews from Russia and 25,000 from Ethiopia arrived in the country. The additional highly skilled labour from Russia led to high growth rates in total output. Figure 8.3 shows a slight

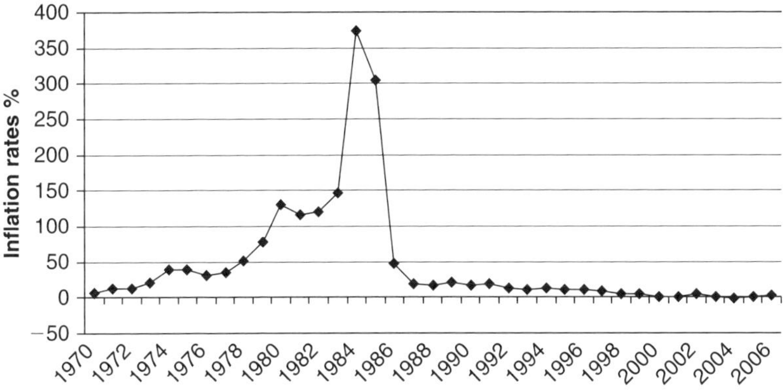

Figure 8.3 The inflation rate in Israel, 1970–2006
Source: World Bank, *World Development Indicators* (April 2008).

improvement of per capita income growth during the early 1990s, but it started to deteriorate again from 1994.

In 1992, the Labour Party won the general election after being in opposition for 15 years. The party came to office at a time of economic recovery, which was augmented by the aforementioned influx of highly skilled labour from Russia. The economic recovery lasted until the middle of the decade. However, the Labour Party also brought back its old labour social policies. In 1993 large wage increases granted to public sector employees (soon emulated by other sectors) led to a substantial rise in private consumption, with important implications for the rate of inflation and imports. By the end of the decade, economic growth had slowed down to less than 3 per cent. At the beginning of the millennium, the country experienced an economic setback and suffered a recession during 2001 and 2002; the important Israeli high-tech industry was hard hit by the slowdown of the IT sector. However, economic recovery had occurred by 2004 and average economic growth until 2006 was approximately 5 per cent.

An important characteristic of the economy of Israel is its isolation from the economies of the MENA region. Israel is a land-locked country with the exception of its Mediterranean coastline in its west. The neighbouring Arab countries have effectively boycotted Israel and its economic relationship with the Arab territories of the West Bank and Gaza Strip has also been marred by repeated border clashes and terrorist attacks. A cursory inspection of Figures 8.1 and 8.2 shows little or no correlation between the economies of Israel and the MENA region. Indeed, statistical correlation between the two is less than 1 per cent. The other important difference between the two economies is that despite poor resources, Israeli per capita income has always been much higher than that of the rest of the region. For instance, in 2006, the Israeli gross national income (GNI) per head was more than eight times the average GNI per capita of the region and 3.7 times the GNI per capita income of Egypt, Jordan and Syria combined. The conclusion from this is that although the economy of Israel has been operating under a state of war, it has benefited from non-regional external forces and its own economic and social management.

Military expenditure

Since its establishment, Israel has gone through five major wars: the war of independence in 1948; the Suez Canal War in 1956; the Six Day War in 1967; the war of attrition with Egypt during 1968–9; and the Yom Kippur War of 1973.

In addition to the above, Israel has also been involved in intermittent wars in Lebanon during 1982 and 2006, various other low-level wars against the Palestinian uprising and skirmishes along its border. The scale and subsequent costs of these wars have been enormous for such a small country. Given the scarcity of its natural resources, any other country in that position would have gone bankrupt without the continuous foreign assistance that Israel has enjoyed. From its inception, Israel was not a capital-poor country. Indeed, the European Jewry who fled before the outbreak of Second World War were well endowed with capital. The Zionist movement was also successful in mobilising support and raising funds for Israel. However, the substantial economic and military assistance which comes from the US has been materially and politically essential for the survival of the state of Israel to an extent that some of the assistance was provided on demand during the crucial stages of wars that Israel has taken part in.

The military success so far of such a small country over its adversaries has been an enigma for many observers and too often portrayed as a myth by Israeli historians. The Arab countries combined have always been able to amass more human and military resources than Israel. Yet they have always been defeated. As discussed earlier, though Israel may be a resource-poor country, it has never lacked the support of powerful foreign powers and has never been a capital-poor country. Therefore, its military expenditure on the wars has been well above its own indigenous resource capabilities and the figures quoted here may well underestimate the true costs of the military in the country.

Military expenditure during the 1970s

At the beginning of the 1970s Israel just came out of the war of attrition with Egypt. The Israeli leaders realised that a prolonged war of attrition was more costly and its outcome less decisive than quick pre-emptive strikes. As discussed earlier, Israel was not endowed with resources to match those of its neighbouring Arab countries. Therefore, the security of the country would be in jeopardy if its hostile neighbours opted for a long-term hostile confrontation. Military expenditure during the 1970s was also influenced by the outcome of the Six Day War in 1967. Israel achieved a sensational victory over its Arab enemies and captured the Sinai Peninsula and Gaza Strip from Egypt, the West Bank from Jordan and the Golan Heights from Syria. The Israeli leaders hoped to eventually trade off these captured territories for peace with the Arab countries. They clearly miscalculated the resolve of the Arab leaders who, facing widespread public anger and discontent because of their miserable performance during the war, had other ideas. The met in Khartoum in 1 September 1967 and issued what is known as the Khartoum Resolution. The Resolution asserted the Arab rejection of the state of Israel and included paragraph 3, which became known as 'the three Nos' – No peace with Israel, No recognition of Israel, and No negotiation with Israel. The Arab leaders also committed themselves to reclaiming the occupied territories by force and reinstating Arab honour and pride.

Consequently, the Six Day War, rather than bolstering Israeli security, in fact put it back on the highest state of alert. The ramifications of the outcome of the war for military expenditure were enormous. The Khartoum Conference also promised much-needed financial assistance to the so-called 'Arab Frontier Countries', of which Egypt was the main beneficiary. The availability of oil finance heightened the arms race in the region, and rivalry between superpowers at the height of the cold war also influenced this arms race.

For Israel, the war had another critical strategic outcome. France ended its strategic co-operation with Israel just days before the outbreak of the war. This left Israel in limbo. Therefore, Israel urgently sought to forge a new strategic alliance with another superpower that guaranteed the supply of military hardware and help for its own military industrialisation. The Israeli leadership was successful in convincing the US of Israel's complementary role to the US's objective of curbing the expansionary fervour of the Soviet Union in the region and that they would also act in accordance with the US interests in the region. The relationship with the US developed at an amazing pace after 1970. Though no explicit defence alliance agreement was signed between the two countries, the US implicitly committed itself to assisting and defending Israel's security and existence.

Table 8.2 shows that the military expenditure represented by its ratio to GDP in 1970 was 23.6 per cent. This represented an increase of 5.5 per cent from its 1967 level. Though this ratio declined slightly in the next two years, the Yom Kippur War increased it to an unprecedented level of 33.3 per cent of GDP. It is worth stating that the data quoted here must be treated with the utmost caution. In most cases it does not cover real costs. For instance, the Yom Kippur War cost Israel the equivalent of one year's GNP and, according to World Bank statistics, this amounted to $5.283bn.

In addition to the security and war problems, the government also faced political problems at home. The economic downturn after the war curtailed the government's ability to raise further funds for defence. To make matters worse, the sudden quadrupling of oil prices engineered by OPEC led to an unprecedented rise in the price of the country's imports.

Table 8.2 Israeli defence expenditure, 1970–9, in $m, at 1978 prices and exchange rates

Year	Military expenditure	Percentage increase	GDP growth rate (%)	ME as percentage of GDP
1970	2,016	–	7.3	23.6
1971	2,166	7.4	11.2	22.8
1972	2,134	−1.5	13.7	20.5
1973	3,880	81.8	3.3	33.3
1974	2,900	−25.3	6.8	–
1975	3,160	9.0	3.3	26.0
1976	3,159	0.0	1.3	26.4
1977	3,079	−2.5	−1.0	24.4
1978	2,676	−13.1	4.8	20.4
1979	2,783	4.0	6.3	20.1
1970–9	27,953			

Note: * estimated.

Sources: World Bank, *World Development Indicators* (April 2008); SIPRI, *Yearbook* (1980, 1981, 1985).

The government subsequently presided over serious budget and balance of payment deficits. The overall economic gloom made raising taxes for further defence spending almost impossible. Subsequently the government resorted to external borrowing to fund its imports as well as its high military expenditure. By 1973, total capital imports into the country amounted to $3.175bn; 68 per cent of these imports were unilateral transfers. During the same year the total debt service burden of the country amounted to $682 million. This burden increased over the years to reach $1.639bn by 1978 (Barnett 1992). Table 8.2 also shows that military expenditure stabilised at around 20 per cent of GDP by the end of the decade. This decline is perhaps the result of a lower level of military hostilities with neighbouring countries, particularly Egypt, which had signed the Camp David Treaty with Israel in 1979.

Military expenditure during the 1980s

Military expenditure remained very high during the 1980s. The extra threat that faced the country was the increasing combat capability of the Palestine Liberation Organisation (PLO) in the late 1970s and 1980s. The organisation made the south of Lebanon its home after its ejection from Jordan in 1970 by King Hussein. It gradually established a

Table 8.3 Israeli defence expenditure, 1980–9, in $m, at 1978 prices and exchange rates

Year	Military expenditure	Percentage increase	GDP growth rate (%)	ME as percentage of GDP
1980	6,110	119.5	6.9	28.2
1981	6,887	12.7	5.2	25.5
1982	7,314	6.2	1.8	24.0
1983	8,000	9.4	3.5	26.1
1984	8,420	5.3	0.9	28.9
1985	5,249	–37.7	3.5	21.1
1986	4,318	–17.7	4.8	16.9
1987	4,134	–4.2	7.2	14.7
1988	3,811	–7.8	2.0	13.0
1989	3,849	1.0	0.9	12.3
1980–9	86,045			

Sources: World Bank, *World Development Indicators* (April 2008); SIPRI, *Yearbook* (1980, 1981, 1988).

formidable militia force in alliance with the Shi'ite Muslims in the south of the country. It also created a virtual state within the state of Lebanon. Frequent incursions into northern Israel also gradually opened another war frontier for the country, which eventually led to the first Israeli war in Lebanon in 1982. As discussed earlier, the war in Lebanon could have become a precursor of an all-out war with Syria, but the Syrian government, fearing isolation from other Arab countries, avoided full military confrontation with Israel, which executed the war and achieved its ultimate aim – the ejection of the PLO from Lebanon.

Table 8.3 shows that military expenditure remained very high until the mid-1980s. The figures show that the country spent an annual average of $8.605bn on its defence. In fact, the highest military expenditure occurred during the lowest period of economic growth, during 1985. Data from WMEAT show that although the conventional army was scaled down gradually, per capita military expenditure remained one of the highest in the world, totalling $2,767 in 1984.

Military expenditure 1990–2006

During the early 1990s, the conventional military race in the region started moving in favour of Israel as Syria lost its most important source of arms; the Soviet bloc. By the mid-1990s most Syrian military equipment became obsolete and the country no longer posed a real threat to Israel in conventional terms. However, as the conventional threats from the neighbouring Arab countries gradually receded the proliferation of weapons of mass destruction started to emerge as a real threat to Israel. Noticeable in this context was the threat from the Islamic regime in Iran. Like Syria, Iran lost its conventional military capability through the war with Iraq and the loss of its traditional source of armaments – the US and Western European countries – after the fall of the Shah's regime in 1979. Subsequently the rulers of both countries shifted their attention to the building up of chemical and biological weapons capabilities as well as clandestinely attempting to acquire nuclear technology and the medium and long-range missiles required for its delivery. Although Israel was widely regarded as a nuclear power, its deterrent capability did not guarantee its peace and security.

Nonetheless, maintaining the country's conventional edge over its neighbours was not cheap. Though the burden of military expenditure in the country has started to ease since the mid-1980s, as Table 8.4 shows, the country still spends a substantial proportion of its GDP on its defence. In real terms, the country still on average spends $8.784bn

Table 8.4 Israeli defence expenditure, 1990–2006, in $m, at 2005 prices and exchange rates

Year	Military expenditure	Percentage increase	GDP growth rate (%)	ME as percentage of GDP
1990	8,003	–	6.8	12.5
1991	10,562	32.0	7.7	15.3
1992	8,425	–20.2	5.6	11.3
1993	8,964	6.2	5.6	11.6
1994	8,267	–7.8	6.9	9.9
1995	8,079	–2.2	6.8	8.7
1996	8,605	6.5	5.6	8.9
1997	8,652	0.0	2.8	8.7
1998	8,981	3.8	4.2	8.6
1999	9,299	3.5	2.9	8.5
1999–9	87,837			
2000	9,574	3.0	8.7	8.0
2001	9,996	4.4	–0.6	8.4
2002	11,087	10.9	–0.9	9.5
2003	10,421	3.0	1.5	8.8
2004	9,931	–4.7	4.8	7.9
2005	10,303	3.7	5.3	7.9
2006	11,076	7.5	5.2	8.0
1990–2006	72,338			

Sources: World Bank, *World Development Indicators* (April 2008); SIPRI, *Military Expenditure Database*.

on its military annually, slightly higher than its average spending during the 1980s. Active Israeli military manpower, by comparison, is still very small. According to Cordesman (2006) it had 141,000 persons under arms in 1991, compared with Syria and Egypt having 404,000 and 448,000 persons under arms respectively. Therefore, in the absence of a comprehensive peace deal with its neighbours, maintaining both its conventional and non-conventional edge is the key to its survival. To do so the country has gradually built a sophisticated military industry, though in collaboration with the US. It is worth mentioning that the costs of building this capability are not included in the data quoted here.

By the beginning of the millennium the defence burden of the country stabilised at around 8 per cent of GDP with an exception in 2002 during which military expenditure as a proportion of GDP increased to 9.5 per cent. In real terms, as Table 8.4 shows, the country on average spent $10.334bn annually during the 2000–6 period.

Conclusion

Israel has been at war or living under the shadow of war since its establishment in 1948. In fact, Jewish people in what is now Israel were at war with the Palestinians and Britain even before the founding of the state of Israel. Its conflict with its neighbours has had profound implications for the geopolitical development of the region. Indeed, many authoritarian and dictatorial Middle Eastern regimes have used the Arab-Israeli conflict as the political pretext for maintaining their grip on power in their countries and subsequently preventing democratic civil institutions from developing. The negative spillover effects of the conflict are clearly manifested in the huge military expenditure and economic stagnation of the region.

The Israeli military expenditure data discussed in this chapter are the monetary measure of just some of the costs; they do not include the full costs of the use of resources involved. In fact there are many hidden costs; some are not accounted for or they are largely underestimated. For instance, they include military assistance from other countries or, indeed, the opportunity costs of engaging civil resources for military conflict. Amongst these is the cost of compulsory service in the IDF, which is three years for men and two years for women. As discussed in Chapter Two, men who are engaged in military service are not just excluded from the production of actual consumer goods but from the consumption of the products of other peoples' labour. Israel also uses highly trained reservists during military operations. This amounts to about 34 days a year for men or more during the immediate conflicts (Sanbar 1990).

Other hidden costs of conflict that are generally underestimated are the loss of output during actual conflicts, the destruction of infrastructure, loss of life and the psychological traumas that the people of the region have had to endure. For instance, as mentioned earlier, the cost of the Yom Kippur War to Israel was equivalent to about one year's gross national income, the costs of Israeli involvement in Lebanon between 1982 and 1985 are estimated to have been about $5bn to the Israeli economy (Rivlin 1992) while the economic costs of that war to the Lebanese economy were estimated to be about $2bn.

The true scale and magnitude of the material costs of the Arab-Israeli conflict are truly immeasurable. The human costs, however, are mostly hidden and continuous. For instance, there are more than three million Palestinians who have been displaced by war and who have been scattered around neighbouring countries. There are generations of Palestinians who have lived in refugee camps without a status or future. Israel refuses to let them return to their homeland under any circumstances.

Perhaps, the most worrying development of the conflict is the competition to acquire nuclear technology by both sides of the conflict. To limit the capability of the other side, Israel bombed and destroyed the Iraqi nuclear installation in Osirak on 7 June 1981, and apparently bombed a Syrian installation in September 2007. Currently, the most dangerous threat to Israel is the current Iranian attempt to develop nuclear technology and the potential threat of it developing a nuclear bomb. The worst scenario, perhaps, is if religious fundamentalist groups develop or acquire such a devastating weapon. Alhough Israel, as mentioned earlier, is widely regarded as having a nuclear capability, the existence of such a deterrent does not eliminate the threat of the further escalation of conflict.

To best means to reduce and ultimately eliminate the threat of further conflict in the region and thereby reduce the burden of military expenditure is to hammer out a credible and long-lasting peace between all the hostile sides. Existing peace agreements between Israel and Egypt are a positive sign, but without a satisfactory solution to the Palestinian problem a comprehensive peace in the region would be still a dream. Peace ultimately requires fundamental compromise from all sides in the conflict. Unfortunately, the current prevailing psychological and political atmosphere does not seem to be conducive to such a long-lasting security settlement.

References

Statistical and primary sources

OPEC (various years) *Annual Statistical Bulletin*, available at: www.opec.org/library/

SIPRI (Stockholm International Peace Research Institute) (various years) *World Armaments and Disarmaments: Yearbooks* (Oxford: Oxford University Press).

SIPRI (Stockholm International Peace Research Institute) (various years) *Military Expenditure Database*, at: www.sipri.org/databases/milex

World Bank (various years) *World Development Indicators* (Washington DC: World Bank Publications); also available by subscription online at: http://publications.worldbank.org/WDI/

UN (United Nations)(various years) *Human Development Reports* (New York: United Nations): at: http://hdr.undp.org/en/reports/

UN (1991) *National Account Statistics: Main Aggregates and Detailed Tables, 1988–89* (New York: United Nations).

WMEAT (*World Military Expenditures and Arms Transfers*) (Washington DC: US Arms Control and Disarmament Agency/US Department of State), various years; some reports available at www.state.gov/t/vci/rls/rpt/wmeat/ and http://dosfan.lib.uic.edu/acda/wmeat95/wmeatpg.htm

Secondary sources

Abu-Qarn, A. S. and S. Abu-Bader (2003) 'Government Expenditure, Military Spending and Economic Growth: Causality Evidence from Egypt, Israel and Syria', *Journal of Policy Modelling*, 25 (6–7), pp. 567–83.

Alami, R. (2002) 'Military Debt: Perspectives from the Experience of Arab Countries', *Defence and Peace Economics*, 13 (10), pp. 13–30.

Al-Marashi and S. Salama (2008) *Iraq's Armed Forces: An Analytical History* (London and New York: Routledge).

Alnasrawi, A. (1994) *The Economy of Iraq* (Westport and London: Greenwood Press).

Al-Yousif, Y. K. (2002) 'Defense Spending and Economic Growth: Some Empirical Evidence From the Arab Gulf Countries', *Defence and Peace Economics*, 13 (3), pp. 187–97.

Amnesty International (1988) *Turkey: Human Rights Denied*, AI Index: EUR/44/65/88, ISBN 086210 156 5, London, November 1988, p. 1.

Amuzegar, J. (1993) *Iran's Economy under the Islamic Republic* (London and New York: I. B. Tauris).

Aronson, S. (2000) 'Israeli Nuclear Programme, the Six Day War and its Ramifications', in Efraim Karsh (ed.), *Israel: The First Hundred Years* (London and Portland: Frank Cass).

Askari, H. and V. Corbo (1974) 'Economic Implications of Military Expenditures in the Middle East', *Journal of Peace Research*, 11 (4), pp. 341–3.

Ball, N. (1983) 'Defense and Development: A Critique of the Benoit Study', *Economic Development and Cultural Change*, 31, pp. 507–24.
Ball, N. (1987) 'Security Expenditure: Measurement and Trends', in S. Deger and R. West (eds), *Defence, Security and Development* (London: Frances Pinter).
Ball, N. (1988) *Security and the Economy in the Third World* (London: Adamantine Press).
Barnett, N. M. (1992) *Confronting the Costs of War: Military Power, State and Society in Egypt and Israel* (Princeton: Princeton University Press).
Bauer, J. (1999) 'Turkey and Greece: A Review of the Defence Economics Literature.' Paper delivered at the Middle Eastern Technical University, Conference III, Ankara, Turkey.
Benoit, E. (1973) *Defence and Economic Growth in Developing Countries* (Boston: Lexington Books).
Benoit, E. (1978) 'Growth and Defence in Developing Countries', *Economic Development and Cultural Change*, 26, pp. 271–80.
Biswas, B. (1993) 'Defense Spending and Economic Growth in Developing Countries', in J. E. Payne and A. P. Sahu (eds), *Defense Spending and Economic Growth* (Boulder: Westview Press).
Biswas, B. and R. Ram (1986) 'Military Expenditure and Economic Growth in Developing Countries: An Augmented Model and Further Evidence', *Economic Development and Cultural Change*, 34 (2), pp. 361–72.
Blackaby, F. and T. Ohlson (1987) 'Military Expenditure and the Arms Trade: Problems of the Data', in C. Schmidt (ed.), *The Economics of Military Expenditures* (Basingstoke: Macmillan).
Bremer, P. (2006) *My Year in Iraq: The Struggle to Build a Future of Hope* (New York: Simon and Schuster).
Brzoska, M. (1981) 'The Reporting of Military Expenditures', *Journal of Peace Research*, 18 (3), pp. 261–75.
Central Bank of Egypt (2006) 'External Position of the Egyptian Economy, Fiscal Year 2005/06', *Quarterly Report*, 14 September.
Central Intelligence Agency (CIA) (1998) *Factbook: Turkey*.
Chowdhury, R. A. (1991) 'A Causal Analysis of Defence Spending and Economic Growth', *Journal of Conflict Resolution*, 35 (1), pp. 80–97.
Chubin, S. (2006) *Iran's Nuclear Ambitions* (Washington DC: Carnegie Endowment for International Peace).
Clements, B., S. Gupta and J. Schiff (1997) 'What Happened to the Peace Dividend?', *Finance and Development*, March 1997, pp. 17–19.
Cohen, J. S. and M. D. Ward (1995) 'Defense Spending, Investment and Peace Dividend: A Look at the Political Economies of Israel and Egypt.' Paper prepared for presentation at the American Political Science Association 1995 Annual Meeting, Chicago.
Cohen, J. S. and M. D. Ward (1996) 'Towards a Peace Dividend in the Middle East: The New Dynamics of Military Expenditure', in N. P. Gleditch, A. Cappelen, O. Bjerkholt, R. Smith and P. Dunne (eds), *The Peace Dividend* (Amsterdam: North Holland)
Cordesman, A. H. (1999a) *Iraq and the War of Sanctions* (Westport and London: Praeger).
Cordesman, A. H. (1999b) *Iran's Military Forces in Transition* (Westport and London: Praeger).

Cordesman, A. H. (2006) *Arab-Israeli Military Forces in an Era of Asymmetric Wars* (Westport: Praeger Security International).

Dagi, I. (1996) 'Democratic Transition in Turkey, 1980–83: The Impact of European Diplomacy', *Middle Eastern Studies*, 32 (2), pp. 124–41.

Davoodi, H., B. Clements, J. Schiff and P. Debaere (1999) 'Military Spending, the Peace Dividend and Fiscal Adjustment', IMF Working Paper WP/99/87 (Washington DC: International Monetary Fund).

Dunne, P. (1996) 'Economic Effects of Military Expenditure in Developing Countries: A Survey', in N. P. Gleditch, A. Cappelen, O. Bjerkholt, R. Smith and P. Dunne (eds), *The Peace Dividend* (Amsterdam: North Holland).

Dunne P., R. Smith and D. Willenbockel (2005) 'Models of Military Expenditure and Growth: A Critical Review, *Defence and Peace Economics*, 16 (6), pp. 449–61.

El-Ghonemy, M. R. (2003) 'Development Strategies, 1950–2001: Progress and Challenges for the Twenty-first Century', in M. R. El-Ghonemy (ed.), *Egypt in the Twenty-First Century: Challenges and Development* (London and New York: RoutledgeCurzon).

Engels, F. (1975) *Anti-Dühring* (London: Lawrence & Wishart).

Filkins, D. (2003) 'Kurds are Finally Heard: Turkey Burned Our Villages', *New York Times*, 24 October.

Fisher, S. N. (ed.) (1963) *The Military in the Middle East* (Columbus: Ohio State University Press).

Frederiksen, P. C. and R. E. Looney (1983) 'Defense Expenditures and Economic Growth in Developing Countries', *Armed Forces and Society*, 9 (Summer), pp. 633–46.

Gabelnick, T. (1999) 'Turkey: Arms and Human Rights', *Foreign Policy Focus*, 4 (16), May.

Gleditch, N. P., A. Cappelen and O. Bjerkholt (1994) *The Wages of Peace: Disarmament in a Small Industrialized Economy* (London: Sage Publications).

Gleditch, N. P., A. Cappelen, O. Bjerkholt, R. Smith and P. Dunne (eds) (1996) *The Peace Dividend* (Amsterdam: Elsevier).

Goldschmidt, A. (1988) *Modern Egypt: The Formation of a Nation State* (Oxford: Westview Press).

Gottheil, F. M. (1974) 'An Economic Assessment of the Military Expenditure Burden in the Middle East: 1969–1980', *The Journal of Conflict Resolution*, 18 (3), pp. 502–13.

Hakimian, H. and M. Karshenas (2000) 'Dilemmas and Prospects for Economic Reform and Reconstruction in Iran', in P. Alizadeh (ed.), *The Economy of Iran* (London and New York: I. B. Tauris).

Hakimian, H. and M. Karshenas (2005) 'Oil, Economic Diversification and Democratic Process in Iran', *Iranian Studies*, 38 (1), pp. 67–90.

Hale, W. (1994) *Turkish Politics and the Military* (London and New York: Routledge).

Halliday, F. (1979) *Iran: Dictatorship and Development*, 2nd edition (Harmondsworth: Penguin Books).

Halliday, F. (2005) *The Middle East in International Relations* (Cambridge: Cambridge University Press).

Hopwood, D. (1988) *Syria 1945–1986: Politics and Society* (London: Unwin Hyman)

Hickman, F. W. (1982) *Ravaged and Reborn: The Iranian Army* (Washington DC: Brookings Institution).

Hinnebusch, R. (2001) *Syrian Revolution from Above* (London: Routledge).

Hinnebusch, R. (2003) 'Globalisation, State Formation and Generation Change: Foreign Policy in Syria and Jordan.' European University Institute Working Paper, RSC No. 2003/19 (Florence: European University Institute).
Hirst, D. (1971) 'The Terror from Tikrit', *The Guardian*, 26 November, p. 15.
Hirst, W. F. (1915) *The Political Economy of War* (London and Toronto: J. M. Dent & Sons).
Ikram, K. (2006) *The Egyptian Economy, 1952–2000* (London and New York: Routledge).
IMF (International Monetary Fund) (2003) *Iraq: Macroeconomic Assessment*, 21 October (Washington DC: IMF).
Jenkins, G. (2001) *Context and Circumstance: The Turkish Military and Politics*, International Institute for Strategic Studies (Oxford: Oxford University Press).
Joerding, W. (1986) 'Economic Growth and Defence Spending', *Journal of Development Economics*, 21 (1), pp. 35–40
Kanovsky, E. (2000) *Syria's Economy: Prospects for Peace, Aid, and Market Reform*, PeaceWatch (2000) #245: Special Forum Report (Washington DC: Washington Institute for Near East Policy).
Karagol, E. (2005) 'Defence Expenditures and External Debt in Turkey', *Defence and Peace Economics*, 16 (2), pp. 117–25.
Karsh, E. (1987) 'Military Power and Foreign Policy Goals: The Iran-Iraq War Revisited', *International Affairs*, 64 (1), pp. 83–95.
Kennedy, G. (1975) *The Economics of Defence* (Totowa: Rowman and Littlefield).
Khadduri, M. (1953) 'The Role of the Military in Middle East Politics', *American Political Science Review*, 47 (2), pp. 511–24.
Khilji, S. M. (2005) 'Military Expenditure and Economic Development: A Comparative Case Study.' Paper presented at the CSID Six Annual Conference, Washington DC, 22–23 April.
Klare, M. (1976) 'Hoist on Your Own Pahlavi', *The Nation*, No. 31, January.
Kusi, K. N. (1994) 'Economic Growth and Defence Spending in Developing Countries: A Causal Analysis', *The Journal of Conflict Resolution*, 38 (1), pp. 152–9.
Landau, D. (1994) 'The Impact of Military Expenditures on Economic Growth on the Less Developed Countries', *Defence and Peace Economics*, 5 (1), pp. 205–20.
Lebovic, J. H. and A. Ishaq (1987) 'Military Burden Security Needs and Economic Growth in the Middle East', *Journal of Conflict Resolution* 31 (1), pp. 106–138.
Lewis, B. (2003) *The Crisis of Islam* (London: Weidenfeld & Nicolson).
Lee, C. (2006) 'Cold War Missiles Target of Blackout', *Washington Post*, 21 August.
Looney, R. E. (1993) 'Government Expenditures and Third World Economic Growth in the 1980s: The Impact of Defense Expenditures', *Canadian Journal of Development Studies*, 14 (1), pp. 23–42.
Looney, R. E. and D. Winterford (1995) *Economic Causes and Consequences of Defense Expenditures in the Middle East and South Asia* (Boulder: Westview Press).
Lebovic, H. J. (1999) 'Using Military Spending Data: "The Complexity of Simple Inference"', *Journal of Peace Research*, 36 (6), pp. 681–97.
Lybyer, A. H. (1913) *Government of the Ottoman Empire in the Age of Suleiman the Magnificent* (Cambridge MA: Harvard University Press).
Molthus, T. (2004[1798]) *'An Essay on the Principle of Population'*, (Oxford: Oxford University Press, Oxford World's Classics).
Marx, K. and F. Engels (1951) *Selected Works*, Volume I (Moscow: Progress Publishers).

Mehring, F. (1962) *Karl Marx, the Story of His Life*, translated by Edward Fitzgerald (Ann Arbor: University of Michigan Press).

Mofid, K. (1990) *The Economic Consequences of the Gulf War* (London and New York: Routledge).

Moran, H. T. (1978) 'Iranian Defense Expenditures and the Social Crisis', *International Security*, 3 (3), pp. 178–92.

Neild, R. (1981) *How to Make Up Your Mind about the Bomb* (London: Andre Deutsch).

Öniş, Z. (1991) 'Political Economy of Turkey in the 1980s', in M. Harper (ed.), *Strong State and Economic Interest Groups: The Post-1980 Turkish Experience* (New York and Berlin: Walter de Gruyter).

OPEC (various years) *Annual Statistical Bulletin*, available at: www.opec.org/library/

Özmucur, S. (1996) 'The Peace Dividend in Turkey', in N. P. Gleditch, A. Cappelen, O. Bjerkholt, R. Smith and P. Dunne (eds), *The Peace Dividend* (Amsterdam: North Holland).

Özsoy, O. (2000) 'The Defence-Growth Relation: Evidence from Turkey', in J. Brauer and Keith Hartley (eds), *The Economics of Regional Security: NATO, the Mediterranean, and Southern Africa* (Amsterdam: Harwood Academic Publishers).

Pigou, A. C. (1921) *The Political Economy of War* (New York: Macmillan and Co. Limited)

Plessner, Y. (1994) *The Political Economy of Israel: From Ideology to Stagnation* (Albany: State University of New York Press).

Reiser, S. (1989) *The Israeli Arms Industry* (New York and London: Holmes & Meier).

Ricardo, D. (1973) *The Principles of Political Economy and Taxation* (London: Everyman's Library).

Ricardo, D. (1820) 'Essay on the Funding System', in P. Sraffa (ed.), *The Works and Correspondence of David Ricardo*, Volume 4, pp. 143–300 (Cambridge: Cambridge University Press).

Rivlin, P. (1992) *The Israeli Economy* (Boulder: Westview Press).

Sanbar, M. (1990) 'The Political Economy of Israel: 1948–1982', in M. Sanbar (ed.), *Economic and Social Policy in Israel: The First Generation* (Lanham, New York and London: University Press of America).

Sandler, T. and K. Hartley (1995) *The Economics of Defense* (Cambridge: Cambridge University Press).

Say, J. B. (1821) *A Treatise on Political Economy*, Volume II, Book III (London: A. and R. Spottiswoode)

Schiff, Z. (1987) *A History of the Israeli Army: 1874 to the Present* (London: Sidgwick & Jackson).

Sen, S. (1992) 'Patterns and Trends in the Military Expenditures of Developing Countries', in Geoffrey Lam and Valeriana Kallab (eds), *Military Expenditure and Economic Development,* World Bank Discussion Paper 185 (Washington DC: World Bank).

Shlaim, A. (2000) *The Iron Wall: Israel and the Arab World* (London: Penguin Books).

Simon, S. R. (2004) *Iraq between the Two World Wars* (New York: Columbia University Press).

Sköns, E. (2002) 'Understanding Military Expenditure: The SIPRI Experience.' Presentation at the Budgeting for Defence in Africa workshop, organised by African Security Dialogue and Research (ASDR), Accra, Ghana, 25–26 February.

Sluglett, P. and M. Rarouk-Sluglett (1990) *Iraq Since 1958: From Revolution to Dictatorship* (London and New York: I. B. Tauris).

Smith, A. (1976) *An Inquiry into the Nature and Causes of the Wealth of Nations*, Volumes 1, II (Indianapolis: Liberty Classics).

Smith, D. and R. Smith (1980) 'Military Expenditure, Resources and Development.' Birkbeck College Discussion Paper No. 87 (London: Birkbeck College).

Smith, R. P. (2000) 'Defence Expenditure and Economic Growth', in N. P. Gleditsch, G. Lindgren, N. Mouhleb, S. Smith and I. de Soysa (eds), *Making Peace Pay: A Bibliography on Disarmament and Conversion* (Laremont: Regina Books), pp. 15–24.

SIPRI (Stockholm International Peace Research Institute) (various years) *World Armaments and Disarmaments: Yearbooks* (Oxford: Oxford University Press).

SIPRI (Stockholm International Peace Research Institute) (various years) *Military Expenditure Database*, at: www.sipri.org/databases/milex

Stork, J. and J. Paul (1983) 'Arms Sales and the Militarization of the Middle East', in *MERIP Reports*, No. 112 (February), *The Arms Race in the Middle East* (Washington DC: MERIP), pp. 5–15.

Tal, D. (2000) 'The Forgotten War: Jewish-Palestinian Strife in Mandatory Palestine, December 1947–May 1948', in Efraim Karsh (ed.), *Israel: The First Hundred Years* (London and Portland: Frank Cass).

Todaro, M. (2000) *Economic Development*, 7th edition (Reading MA and Amsterdam: Addison-Wesley).

Torrey G. H. (1964) *Syrian Politics and the Military 1945–1958* (Columbus: Ohio State University Press).

United Nations, *National Account Statistics: Main Aggregates and Detailed Tables, 1988–89* (New York: United Nations).

US Military Sales to Iran: A Staff Report (1976) Printed for the use of the Committee on Foreign Relations, July 1976 (Washington DC: US Government Printing Office).

Utkulu, U. (2001) 'The Turkish Economy: Past and Present', in D. Lovatt (ed.), *Turkey since 1970* (New York: Palgrave).

Vatikiotis, P. J. (1961) *The Egyptian Army in Politics* (Westport: Greenwood Press).

Washington Post (2006), 21 August edition.

Williamson, J. and C. Milner (1991) *The World Economy* (New York and London: Harvester Wheatsheaf).

WMEAT (2001) *World Military Expenditure and Arms Transfers 1999–2000* (Washington DC: US Department of State), October.

WMEAT (2003) *World Military Expenditure and Arms Transfers 1989–99* (Washington DC: US Department of State), February.

World Bank (various issues) *World Development Indicators* (Washington DC: World Bank Publications); also available online at: http://publications.worldbank.org/WDI/

World Bank (2008) *Global Development Finance Report* (Washington DC: World Bank).

Yapp, M. E. (1996) *The Near East since the First World War: A History to 1995* (Harlow: Longman).

Yildirim, J., S. Sezgin and N. Ocal (2005) 'Military Expenditure and Economic Growth in Middle Eastern Countries: A Dynamic Panel Data Analysis', *Defence and Peace Economics*, 16 (4), pp. 283–95.

Zisser, E. (2001) 'The Syrian Army: Between the Domestic and External Fronts', *Middle East Review of International Affairs*, 5 (1), pp. 1–7.

Index